I0189722

**Student Centered, Innovation Driven**

# STUDENT CENTERED, INNOVATION DRIVEN

## A Guide to Transforming Higher Education

RICHARD D. MUMA

University Press of Kansas

© 2025 Richard D. Muma and Wichita State University
Third Printing

Published by the University Press of Kansas (Lawrence, Kansas 66045), which was
organized by the Kansas Board of Regents and is operated and funded by Emporia
State University, Fort Hays State University, Kansas State University, Pittsburg State
University, the University of Kansas, and Wichita State University.

Library of Congress Cataloging-in-Publication Data

Names: Muma, Richard D. author
Title: Student centered, innovation driven : A guide to transforming
higher education / Richard D. Muma.
Description: Lawrence : University Press of Kansas, [2025] | Includes
bibliographical references and index.
Identifiers: LCCN 2025019525 (print) | LCCN 2025019526 (ebook) |
ISBN 9780700640652 cloth | ISBN 9780700640669 ebook
Subjects: LCSH: Student-centered learning | Education, Higher—Technological
innovations | Wichita State University—Administration | Universities and
colleges—United States—Administration | Educational change—United States |
BISAC: EDUCATION / Administration / Higher
Classification: LCC LB1027.23 .M86 2025 (print) | LCC LB1027.23 (ebook)
| DDC 378.1/070973—dc23/eng/20250618
LC record available at https://lccn.loc.gov/2025019525.
LC ebook record available at https://lccn.loc.gov/2025019526.

British Library Cataloguing-in-Publication Data is available.
Authorised Representative Details: Easy Access System Europe
Mustamäe tee 50, 10621 Tallinn, Estonia | gpsr.requests@easproject.com

To all the presidents of Wichita State University who have come before me: Your vision, leadership, and commitment have built the foundation of this institution's success. It is my honor and privilege to follow in your footsteps.

And to the first First Gentleman of Wichita State University, Rick Case, whose unwavering support and encouragement have always been my greatest source of strength.

# Contents

· · · · · · · · · · · · · · · · · · · · · · · · · · · · · · · · · · · · · · · · · · · · · · · · · · ·

# Preface

· · · · · · · · · · · · · · · · · · · · · · · · · · · · · · · · · · · · · · · · · · · · · · · · · · · · · · · ·

There's no shortage of metrics to measure a university's success: acceptance rates, research awards, alumni earnings, and graduation and retention rates, to name a few. But university presidents and administrators across the nation will tell you that it's their current and future enrollment numbers that keep them up at night, especially with the enrollment cliff the United States is experiencing.[1]

Wichita State University (WSU) has been celebrating record enrollment at a time when many educational institutions are starting to see declines.[2] Our work from across the university aims to continue our increases while acknowledging the challenges ahead that could make this difficult.

The National Science Foundation has listed the university in the top ten for engineering research and development among all colleges and universities in the nation and as No. 1 for aerospace research and development expenditures.[3] These rankings reinforce our reputation as a leader in applied research and innovation, making Wichita State an attractive destination for students seeking hands-on learning experiences and strong industry connections. By securing significant research funding and fostering partnerships with global leaders in aerospace, manufacturing, and technology, we provide students with real-world opportunities that enhance their education and career prospects—key factors in our continued enrollment growth.

The upswing in enrollment and research rankings over the past several years seems to be a harbinger of good news—particularly for a midsize research university in the Midwest and in a state with minimal growth in its population. But in my thirty-five-plus years in higher education, I have learned that it's never wise to get too comfortable resting on your laurels.

## BORN TO BE A SHOCKER

More than fifty years before I became president of WSU, I was a little kid running through campus, visiting my grandparents who worked there—my grandmother (Mary Blowers) as a secretary in the philosophy department and my grandfather (Edward Blowers) as a purchasing director.

I was born in Wichita, Kansas, and grew up in Houston, Texas, but I remained connected to Wichita State's news and events through my family, some of whom are proud Shocker alums.[4]

In the 1980s, I went to school at the University of Texas Medical Branch (UTMB) in Galveston, Texas, and eventually became a physician assistant (PA), specializing in internal medicine and infectious diseases. I practiced there during the

Mary and Edward Blowers, President Muma's grandparents, worked for Wichita State University from the
1950s to 1980s.

very early days of the HIV/AIDS epidemic. It was a tumultuous time to be a health care professional. There was so much
uncertainty, fear, misinformation, and unbearable loss, as well
as some of the uglier manifestations of the HIV crisis: judg-
ment and ignorance. Not that much different from the recent
COVID-19 pandemic.

It was during this era of my career that I focused on public health—researching patient behaviors for practitioners to understand why patients choose to engage in risky behaviors. Obviously, that level of understanding can guide health care professionals in designing or modifying treatment plans and other interventions to improve patients' outcomes.

Health care, I tell people, is so much more than easing physical suffering. It's about listening, understanding, and bridging the gap between being a patient and being a person.

I've drawn on that experience to guide my efforts in advancing Wichita State, fostering a culture where listening and understanding drive meaningful progress.

In my current role as president of Wichita State, I've swapped patients for students, faculty, and staff, but the same concept still applies: People are complex. They are more than their symptoms, their majors, their jobs, or their situation. Each has their own story or their own reason why.

Throughout my time at UTMB, WSU was always in my periphery, and in the mid-1990s, I returned to Wichita—this time as a professor in the PA department, eventually becoming department chair, and then chair in public health sciences. Apart from my time in Galveston and a two-year stint as director of the Saint Louis University PA program, I've spent my career at Wichita State University.

Over time, it became clear that I had interest in the organizational details of academia—bridging the big picture with the mechanics of getting it done.

Over the next several years, I moved up the administrative ladder, eventually being named as an associate vice president in charge of enrollment, assessment, and accreditation and then provost of the university. Through all these experiences, I had a unique view of the university, seeing it change over time and having been intimately involved in many of those changes and in shaping its future.

In late 2020, the Kansas Board of Regents, the governing body for WSU, began its search for Wichita State's next president. It was an opportunity I hadn't given much consideration throughout the course of my career, and I dedicated careful thought to whether I would be the right leader at the right time. After much deliberation, I threw my hat into the ring.[5]

On May 6, 2021, the Kansas Board of Regents appointed me as the fifteenth president of Wichita State University. It was an incredible honor and a once-in-a-lifetime opportunity —one that seemed improbable given my background as a physician assistant, a role not traditionally associated with university leadership. Yet, this appointment marked a turning point, allowing me to build on the strong foundation laid by my predecessors while bringing a unique perspective to the presidency.[6] Now I had the opportunity to build on the momentum of those earlier leaders.

Speaking of my predecessors, one president in particular, Dr. John Bardo, the thirteenth president at Wichita State, played a pivotal role in helping the university transform into what it is today. You will read a lot about him in the coming chapters. This coverage of him and his vision in no way diminishes the role of the approximately five thousand employees of the university and their significant contributions to the transformation.

I decided to tell this story for a couple of reasons: First, 2024 marked ten years since the establishment of our Innovation Campus, an addition that set into motion our transformation as a university. Second, I think that my fifty-plus-year connection to Wichita State gives me a unique front-row seat and credibility to tell the contemporary story of Wichita State. It needs to be told, so here goes.

## A NOTE TO THE READER

It is with great enthusiasm that we present this book and introduce you to the remarkable institution that's been part of my life for more than half a century. Please be advised that the facts and information presented herein are true at the time of publication. My team and I have diligently researched and verified each detail to provide you with the most up-to-date and accurate representation possible. However, it's important to recognize that the world is ever-changing, and political and governmental influences, in addition to new discoveries and developments, are emerging as this book is being published.

# Introduction

· · · · · · · · · · · · · · · · · · · · · · · · · · · · · · · · · · · · · · · · · · · · · · · · · · · · ·

L eading a public university means navigating a constant flow of perspectives on the future of higher education. It comes at you from all directions: regents, the board of trustees, the state legislature, our students, faculty and staff, social media, reporters, passersby on the street, and friends and family.

Frankly, it's overwhelming, and there's an urge to discount it all as armchair quarterbacking. But listen carefully and objectively, and you're likely to learn more about your institution, your community and its needs, and your role as an educational leader.

In an ever-evolving world, especially politically, higher education is facing unprecedented challenges, and everyone is looking for answers. The demands of the modern era require a dynamic response from universities and colleges, pushing them to adapt and transform to remain relevant to society's needs.

This book is not another collection of random suggestions or idealistic theories. Instead, it is a warts-and-all story about the hard-fought transformation of Wichita State University— from a small educational institution in middle America to one that has cultivated a thriving culture and campus around innovation and community engagement.

My guess is that this book will be of most interest to higher education professionals seeking insights into how we traversed our journey. However, each institution has its own story, and this book aims to help readers wholly embrace that identity, build community around their own traditions and innovations, and grow to achieve each institution's potential.

As you think about your own transformative journey, remember that change is not a single event. Rather, it's a continuous process. It requires commitment, resilience, appropriate risk, and a willingness to embrace uncertainty. With this book, you are invited to explore how to transform your institution into a dynamic hub of entrepreneurship, innovation, and exponential growth.

Whether you are a seasoned university leader seeking new insights or a rising administrator preparing to take the reins, let us embrace the possibilities of change together and rise above the overwhelming noise, propelling our institutions into a brighter and more promising future.

The sharing of our journey begins now.

................................................................

## What to Expect in This Book

We'll embark on an exploration of the remarkable evolution Wichita State University has undergone during the past decade and previously. Before we dive into the details, let's take a moment to understand the format you can expect as you proceed through the book. Beginning in chapter 2, each chapter starts with a brief introduction, providing a snapshot of the key highlights and themes that will be explored in depth. These introductions are designed to set the stage for the insightful discussions that follow.

# 1

## Who Is Wichita State University?

The university . . . needs to take a role in strengthening local companies so that our graduates can be employed here.

Even further back than my personal connections, Wichita State carries its own institutional memories—130 years of providing educational opportunities for students and reaching beyond the borders of our campus to meet the needs of the community. Our faculty members and researchers are engaged with the people of our state to learn how we can build solutions for them.

We are Kansas's only urban public research university, focused on being student centered and innovation driven,[1] which means we prioritize both access to education and real-world preparedness for our students. Being student centered means meeting students where they are, providing flexible pathways to degrees, embedding applied learning into every program, and ensuring that our graduates leave with the skills and experiences necessary to thrive in their careers. Being innovation driven means that we continually evolve our teaching, research, and industry partnerships to meet the demands of a rapidly changing world, fostering an entrepreneurial mindset and equipping students with the tools to drive progress.

Our location in the heart of Kansas's most populous city—and one of the state's most diverse communities[2]—is one of our greatest advantages. It brings with it a variety of cultures, races, social and economic experiences, and faiths. This array of diversity generates a wealth of opportunity, and it's a guiding star on our path to achieving excellence.

Since its founding as Fairmount College in 1895, Wichita State has built its home at 1845 Fairmount Street around three foundational tenets: access to higher education, innovation, and a commitment to community.[3] Though the definition and implementation of those things have evolved in the past century, the strength of Shocker Nation rests solidly and resolutely on those guiding principles.

In 1926, Fairmount College became the Municipal University of Wichita, making it the first of its kind west of the Mississippi River.[4] Then, in 1964, the University of Wichita became Wichita State University, one of the six state-supported universities in Kansas.[5]

The university enjoyed steady growth throughout the next three decades, reaching its peak at 17,419 students in 1989. That is until 2023, when WSU surpassed that number with 17,548 students on the main campus and 5,655 at WSU Tech[6] for a total of 23,203, followed by 2024, when we reached an enrollment of 23,806 students.[7]

Despite our successes in the late 1980s, in the following decades Wichita State University faced several challenges. The university was not growing, needed additional degree programming, and had dramatic cuts in state funding—all of which, unfortunately, perpetuated a reputation among the community of it being merely a convenient and unremarkable option for locals to earn a degree.

The university's student demographics were also beginning to change, making WSU the most diverse university in the state. As of the publication of this book:

- Thirty-nine percent of our students identify as a minority.[8]
- Forty-two percent of our students are eligible for a Pell Grant.[9]
- Eighteen percent of the undergraduate population identifies as Hispanic,[10] resulting in the university being categorized as an emerging Hispanic Serving Institution.[11]
- Nearly half of the undergraduate student body are first-generation students.[12]

With that celebrated growth in diversity also came new challenges for students who struggled to afford and succeed in college. Reputational issues, declining state funding, and underresourced students began to weigh heavily on the university.

Perhaps more crucially, society's expectations of what a public university ought to do were shifting. In the past, universities were often seen primarily as institutions for academic knowledge and intellectual growth, and the focus was primarily on acquiring theoretical knowledge. Over time, there have been higher expectations for universities to provide knowledge, skills, and experiences that directly translate to the job market.

Wichita State University understood the challenges we were facing but also saw opportunities to differentiate: to position

Fairmount College, ca. 1912. In this panoramic photo, Fairmount College students, faculty, and staff stand in front of (from left to right) Fairmount Hall, Morrison Library, the Knickerbocker House, and Fiske Hall. Photo courtesy of WSU Libraries.

ourselves for growth through access and affordability, to provide our community and state with a talent pipeline by focusing on experiential learning, or what we commonly call applied learning, and by increasing economic prosperity for our community.[13]

## A DIFFERENT WAY FORWARD

When Dr. John Bardo was selected as Wichita State's thirteenth president in 2012, he brought with him a bold vision that led

to the creation of the WSU Innovation Campus and a plan to immerse our students in a new model for applied learning and a research curriculum that would prepare them for the careers of the future. On-campus, work-based learning wasn't an entirely new concept for WSU. The university had been engaged in providing students with employment opportunities from the very beginning, when—for extra money—students shocked wheat in adjacent farm fields, although this specific work was not necessarily connected to their major.[14]

Bardo had been a faculty member at Wichita State from 1976 to 1983, when he taught sociology. He eventually left after being awarded a Fulbright scholarship to study in Australia. In 1995, he was named chancellor of Western Carolina University (WCU), and he spent sixteen years guiding that university

Dr. John Bardo,
thirteenth president
of Wichita State
University.

through an era marked by consistent enrollment growth and a
surge in campus building development.[15]

Like me, he always kept his eye on Wichita State University.
He recognized its potential, and he saw an opportunity to address the challenges the university was facing by reimagining
the many assets and resources it already had at its fingertips—
specifically WSU's National Institute for Aviation Research
(NIAR), the aerospace manufacturing industry in Wichita,
and the university's position as the state's only urban public
research university. He was also aware of Wichita's entrepreneurial past, which includes Cessna, Beechcraft, Pizza Hut,
Rent-A-Center, Koch Industries, Freddy's Frozen Custard and

Steakburgers, and White Castle, among other companies that were founded there. A significant number of the airplanes you fly on, and many of the parts for those planes, are also built in Wichita. In 2019, Bardo detailed these sentiments in an article in *Issues in Science and Technology*: "Innovations in industries as diverse as aviation, energy and fast food have come from Wichita, Kansas, and can continue to do so. At Wichita State University (WSU), we are trying hard to help spur competitiveness, and we have charted a path that is focused on delivering higher education deeply grounded in applied learning and research."[16] That vision Bardo held of innovation and community commitment represented a reawakening for Wichita State and a transition from a university struggling to stay relevant to one that is a thriving model for innovation and an anchor institution for the city of Wichita and the entirety of Kansas.

Upon Bardo's arrival at Wichita State, I was the associate vice president for academic affairs. With my background in public health, the idea of working in collaboration with industry and the community was second nature to me. Throughout my professional training and then my time building programs within Wichita State's College of Health Professions, I worked with hospitals, medical groups, and community organizations in both clinical and educational settings.

Even more so, I was fully on board with Bardo's proposed model for applied learning and research, one where students work side by side with seasoned professionals in their chosen field so that, upon graduation, they're able to make meaningful and immediate contributions to their employers.

As a health care practitioner, I grew up in this world of experiential, hands-on learning. A typical scenario of learning in a health care setting requires students to see one, do one, teach one. As a future physician assistant, I was often thrown into the deep end of patient care in Galveston and Houston, whether it was delivering babies or treating patients with HIV. That immersive experience brought to life what I'd learned from books and in the classroom in a way that built my confidence and bridged my theoretical understanding with professional practice.

It's a model that creates a comprehensive and intensive applied education for students, and it significantly reduces employers' costs in onboarding and training new, less prepared employees.[17]

Bardo also recognized that one of the most significant challenges facing Kansas was the continued out-migration of educated workers and jobs. This was a problem he felt Wichita State could dig its teeth into, as he explained in his article in *Issues in Science and Technology*: "The university . . . needs to take a role in strengthening local companies so that our graduates can be employed here. The university has therefore worked systematically to expand the opportunities for those students . . . to remain in the region."[18] With that in mind, Bardo set to work on selling his big idea to Wichita: the creation of the Wichita State University Innovation Campus, an innovation and research park that would amplify our partnerships with the businesses and industries of our region, create an incubator for applied research and learning that would prepare students for the careers of tomorrow, and nurture a talent pipeline that would create an agile and highly skilled workforce to meet employers' needs and support the economic prosperity of our state.

## BUILDING THE VISION

Today, Wichita State's Innovation Campus is a bastion of enterprise, entrepreneurship, and discovery. Its numerous buildings house private businesses, government agencies, research labs and infrastructure, and advanced facilities that drive idea creation and interdisciplinary problem-solving. It certainly wasn't built in a day, but thanks to bold visionaries and their relentless pursuit of progress, it has exceeded every expectation and continues to transform what's possible.

While the realization of WSU's Innovation Campus included a plethora of moving parts and an enthusiastic group of people dedicated to making it happen, there were two vital Wichita State assets that fueled the manifestation of the Innovation Campus and the university's vision of creating an innovation ecosystem with public-private partnerships.

First, in 1967, the Wichita State Board of Trustees purchased the Crestview Country Club and Golf Course, a 120-acre plot of land contiguous to the main campus.[19] While the golf course, which had been renamed Braeburn Golf Course, continued to be operated, university administration later believed that the Innovation Campus would be a more effective use for that property.

Second, the National Institute for Aviation Research was established at Wichita State University in 1985 to increase research and development (R&D) capabilities and address many of the R&D needs of Wichita's aviation industry. While NIAR is heavily focused on aerospace, it's not tied to any specific academic department. From its beginnings, it has had a history of collaborating with both academia and private businesses. This was integral as the university began to navigate public-private partnerships for the Innovation Campus.

Even with leadership's determination to build the Innovation Campus, to many, the idea felt herculean and just shy of impossible. It might have been expected at a larger research university but not at WSU, which led to growing pains and pushback. One community member wrote in a letter to the editor to *The Wichita Eagle*, "This innovation campus, if it even comes to full fruition, will benefit a very limited number of students."[20] I can look back at comments like that now with a sense of accomplishment, knowing, in fact, that thousands of students have benefited from the Innovation Campus and our student-centered, innovation-driven approach. In 2024, more than nine thousand students earned over $35 million in salaries and benefited from on-campus jobs, co-ops, internships, and applied learning positions.[21]

Between the introduction of the Innovation Campus plan and the plan's realization, there were years of work laying down the infrastructure and preparing the property for its eventual use.

2012 Google Earth image of Wichita State University's campus.

2023 Google Earth image of Wichita State University's campus.

The John Bardo Center, originally named the Experiential Engineering Building, was the first building to open on Wichita State's Innovation Campus.

Finally, in 2015, Wichita State University broke ground on what was then known as the Experiential Engineering Building. The 143,000-square-foot building opened in 2017, standing three stories high and containing dozens of labs and a massive makerspace called GoCreate, a Koch collaborative, which is open to the public.

After Bardo's death in 2019, the building was renamed the John Bardo Center. It remains a symbolic and literal cornerstone of Wichita State's Innovation Campus and the beginnings of the transformation of WSU into a premier urban, public research university.

Soon after, more buildings were erected, and more partners signed on to become part of the innovation ecosystem that

# Wichita State University Innovation Campus Partners

Wichita State's Innovation Campus has an ever-growing list of partnerships with global, national and regional brands that have chosen to locate operations here. These brands reflect some of WSU's Innovation Campus partnerships at the time of publication. For a full list of current Innovation Campus partners, visit *wichita.edu/innovationcampus*.

Wichita State was building—including Airbus, Spirit Aero-Systems, Textron Aviation, The Smart Factory by Deloitte @ Wichita, NetApp, Dassault Systèmes, the Law Enforcement Training Center, and the Bureau of Alcohol, Tobacco, Firearms and Explosives, among many others.

The Innovation Campus is a richly diverse mix of industry and agency partnerships, offering immersive applied learning and research opportunities, many of which are available to our students from day one of their first year. While many of these jobs are wonderful for building résumés, most of them are also paid, helping students offset the cost of higher education and living expenses, as well as get their foot in the door at the onset of their career.

## THE EVOLUTION OF EXCELLENCE

As part of Wichita State's broader transformation, the university saw a significant enhancement in its academic landscape with the establishment of the Dorothy and Bill Cohen Honors College. Under the leadership of its inaugural dean, Dr. Kimberly Engber, the Honors College—which was formalized in 2013 during President Bardo's tenure—has become a critical component of Wichita State's commitment to academic excellence and student success.

The idea of an honors college was conceived as a means to bolster the university's academic reputation and offer a distinctive experience to high-achieving students. The process of creating the college was highly collaborative, engaging students, faculty, and staff from across the campus. Dean Engber, who had been involved since 2012 as program director of the honors program, recalled the excitement and energy surrounding its development: "Creating the Honors College was a collaborative, energizing experience. Students researched models at other institutions, and faculty pushed our model by asking—what will it matter to have an honors college on our campus? The entire process was a tremendous learning experience, and it was thrilling to see so many ideas come to life."[22]

The college built on the university's history of excellence in academia, evolving from a small honors program that had existed since 1957. By the time it became a formal college in 2013, it embodied a renewed vision for higher learning at Wichita State. Dean Engber noted that the honors program was one of the earliest in the country, originally named after Emory Lindquist,[23] a Rhodes Scholar and the first president of Wichita State after it became a state university. This historical foundation helped shape the Honors College into a space where students could engage deeply with their education, blending rigorous academics with opportunities for applied learning, research, and leadership.

Dean Engber emphasized the importance of the Honors College as a critical element of the university's mission to provide access and opportunity to all students, stating, "The Honors College tells students that we believe in their abilities and dreams, and we want to give them all the tools and opportunities to achieve their ambitions."[24]

Dr. Emory K. Lindquist, eighth president of Wichita State University.

The Honors College has quickly become a hallmark of Wichita State's academic offerings, providing students with seminar courses, research opportunities, and leadership programs. All honors students are expected to actively participate in shaping their education, whether through research, internships, study abroad, or turning a regular course into an honors course with additional academic work. The founding of the Honors College aligned perfectly with the broader institutional focus on innovation and academic distinction, mirroring the university's commitment to fostering applied learning and community engagement across all disciplines.

By 2014, the Honors College had formalized its guiding principles in a student-drafted charter, which outlined its vision as follows: "We, the students and faculty, who value the life of the mind, the execution of good work for its own sake, and the common threads uniting every discipline . . . hereby establish an Honors College at Wichita State University."[25]

This formal establishment marked the beginning of a new era for honors education at Wichita State. The college, with its emphasis on creativity, inquiry, and interdisciplinary collaboration, further reinforced the university's evolution toward a more innovative and student-centered institution.

## BUCKING THE TREND

In the early days of September 2024, I bustled through my busy new-semester schedule—faculty gatherings, student luncheons, Shocker athletic events, alumni and donor dinners, and strategic planning meetings. But the impending announcement of our student headcount lurked at the edges of my mind. With every ping from my phone, I felt hopeful that this would be the text or email with the official fall 2024 enrollment numbers. Who am I kidding? I knew where we were in every sector of our market. I knew exactly what the numbers would be. I regularly pored over them with my staff in painstaking detail.

And as I waited, I thought of how remarkable Wichita State's transformation in the past decade had been—from a mostly commuter university to this: a thriving, urban institution, drawing students and talent from across the globe.

Since the establishment of the Innovation Campus, Wichita State has been on a steady incline in enrollment numbers. In fact, other than a slight dip in 2020 due to the COVID-19 pandemic, enrollment has increased each year.[26]

Back in 2021, when many universities were grappling with a continued post-COVID downturn in their student populations, Wichita State University quietly celebrated a 3.5 percent increase.

Then it happened again in 2022, with a 5.1 percent increase—perhaps a little less quietly. Then again in 2023.

My hope was that 2024 would prove that the past few years weren't a fluke but instead were irrefutable evidence that Wichita State is doing the right things for the right reasons. It wasn't a fluke.

To be continued . . .

........................................................................

### What to Expect in Chapter 2

Even under the best of circumstances, change is difficult. Institutional change is, frankly, agonizing, and it requires a tolerance for pain, a stubborn willingness, and a fierce conviction that today's adversities will be tomorrow's victories. This chapter chronicles a vision for Wichita State University, and I'll make no claim that this was, or is, an easy process.

# 2

## A Bold Vision, a Shared Vision

Change is never easy, and these were tumultuous days
for Wichita State.

Wichita State University has undergone a remarkable transformation over the past decade from a regional research institution to an urban public research university powerhouse. Shocker Nation reimagined its potential, reconnected with its community, and built a thriving culture around innovation and opportunity. This transformation was not without growing pains or resistance, but with fierce determination and visionary leadership, the university leaned into the discomfort and fearlessly embarked on a journey toward a new era of excellence.

As mentioned earlier, it's impossible to talk about Wichita State University's transformation without talking about Dr. John Bardo. Dr. Bardo, president of the university from 2012 to 2019, was a visionary. And I don't mean that in a generic sense that he had a great idea. I mean that he saw in Wichita State the potential for a new way forward that would expand the university's impact on its students and community while creating a new model for higher education.

Dr. Donald Beggs, twelfth president of Wichita State University.

While Bardo's vision transformed the university, I want to provide a brief interlude to say that his predecessors played important roles in making Wichita State University the exemplary institution it is today.

One of Bardo's predecessors, Dr. Donald Beggs (WSU's president from 1999 to 2012), was integral in strengthening connections among the university and its surrounding neighborhoods, believing strongly in a symbiotic community-university relationship, as Beggs told a reporter for *The Wichita Eagle* in a 2011 news conference: "The only reason Wichita State University exists is because of Wichita."[1] Because of that relationship, Beggs spent his presidency honoring those roots and consistently creating and fostering connections with the community. Beggs's time at Wichita State was marked by several construction projects. Under his leadership, WSU built the Marcus Welcome Center as the front door for prospective students, built the Engineering Research Building (later renamed Beggs Hall), and made significant improvements to Charles Koch Arena, where today's Shocker basketball and volleyball teams still play. Don and his wife, Shirley, were well-liked among students, faculty, and staff, and the two were often seen at athletic events, chatting with students at the Rhatigan Student Center (WSU's student union), or helping students move into the residence halls at the beginning of the semester.

Also under Beggs's leadership, Wichita State increased funding for research, earning the university a second-place ranking by the National Science Foundation in industry-funded aerospace research.[2] The ranking reflected the mission and efforts of WSU's National Institute for Aviation Research (NIAR) "to strengthen university research capabilities; provide applied learning opportunities for students; and support the aviation and manufacturing industries — while driving innovation and prosperity for the community, region and state."[3]

And while much will be said in the coming chapters about the transformation that John Bardo introduced to Wichita State, it's important to give due credit to President Beggs—and the eleven presidents before him. As the fifteenth president of the university, I am privileged to stand on the shoulders of all of them.

## FROM TRANSACTIONAL TO TRANSFORMATIONAL

Bardo was introduced to Wichita State as a sociology faculty member from 1976 to 1983. He moved on as a Fulbright Scholar conducting research in Australia and eventually landed at Western Carolina University (WCU) in 1995 as chancellor. Bardo's WCU successes included record enrollment, fourteen new or renovated buildings—including the construction of five new residence halls, a campus rec center, a performing arts center that bears his name, and an applied-technology center—as well as the Millennial Initiative, a legacy, and pathway for the university to grow its research through public and private partnerships.[4]

Bardo arrived at Wichita State in 2012 to an institution with declining enrollment, reduced state funding, and hunger for purpose to propel us forward. As much as Beggs moved the university to reconnect with Wichitans, industry connection needed strengthening. The university was also viewed as the easy choice for local high school seniors and adults seeking continuing education but was not necessarily a highly sought-after university. WSU chief of staff Zach Gearhart, a 2011/2013 graduate and former student body president, explained, "We really didn't have a lot happening with industry or government. Most students would drive and park, go to class . . . you might stay for lunch on a long day, but then you would just go home. It was very transactional."[5]

That narrative changed under Bardo's leadership. With a record of making big changes while at WCU, Bardo saw an opportunity to create an innovation ecosystem at Wichita State—one marked with exponential growth in enrollment, the infrastructure of the university, and industry and government partnerships, as well as firmly planting WSU's footprint on Kansas's employment and economic landscape.

Upon taking up the office of the presidency, Bardo placed a big red "yes" button on his desk and assigned his executive team to read *Getting to Yes*, a book about negotiating solutions that benefit all parties.[6] Positive risk-taking became the new expectation, recalled Lou Heldman, who served as Bardo's vice president of the Office of Strategic Communications: "He believed the university had become too cautious," Heldman said, and Bardo wanted to create "a place where ideas were allowed to fully flourish."[7] And to flourish, the university needed a road map to show where we were, where we wanted to be, and how to get there.

Simply put, we needed a strategic plan. "This was Wichita State putting our flag in the ground and saying, 'This is what we stand for, and this is what we aspire to be,'" said now-retired, then marketing professor at WSU Cindy Claycomb.[8] Claycomb cochaired the Strategic Planning Steering Committee with Ed O'Malley, then-CEO of the Kansas Leadership Center and current CEO of the Kansas Health Foundation. In 2012, the committee kicked off the university's strategic planning process with a retreat at WSU's Charles Koch Arena,[9] where more than four hundred people from across campus and the greater Wichita community gathered.

At the retreat, Bardo presented information on the

challenges of higher education and asked participants to discuss key areas of focus for the university: values, mission, strengths, weaknesses, threats, opportunities, obstacles, and goals. After a lengthy discussion, each group presented a key idea that emerged. Hundreds of ideas, opportunities, and challenges surfaced. More important, the university engaged with members of the community, listened to their input, and created a path forward where their voices were heard and valued. As Claycomb saw it, this was a chance for everyone to get excited about the future of the university: "We wanted to let them know that we really are building a strategic plan, and it's really going to include everyone. If you want to be involved, you can be involved."[10] There were many opportunities beyond this kickoff event to be included in the planning process. Throughout campus, Bardo and his leadership team continually sought suggestions about the future from students, faculty, and staff.

The Strategic Planning Steering Committee, composed of more than thirty staff and faculty from across campus, hosted four public town hall events, seventeen breakfast meetings with university leadership, four roundtable discussions with key groups on campus, and twenty-five meetings with Wichita State centers and institutes.

For his part, Bardo was consistent in his message to the campus and the broader community: WSU's core purpose is to improve lives. From his first year, he launched a strategic planning process grounded in an ambitious vision—to position WSU as an internationally recognized model for applied learning and research. This vision was paired with a mission to serve as an essential educational, cultural, and economic driver for Kansas and the broader public good. The words *economic driver* were of particular importance within the statement, as it's not often that universities so explicitly highlight their role in economic development. Yet, it's crucial to showcase how universities like WSU not only educate students but also contribute to the broader prosperity of their regions.

Bardo began assessing Wichita State's potential at a time when community leaders were also asking hard questions about the city—to which Bardo was listening. Wichita State leadership began collaborating in 2015 with the Greater Wichita Partnership to build the Blueprint for Regional Economic Growth (BREG). The partnership engaged leaders in ten counties, several government agencies,[11] and multiple private businesses to study the opportunities, strengths, and challenges of the region and to create a framework for growth. Seven sectors of opportunity were identified by the partnership: advanced manufacturing, aerospace, agriculture, data services and IT, transportation and logistics, energy, and health care.[12]

Around the same time, the Wichita Foundation engaged James Chung and his company, New York–based Reach Advisors, to help navigate the path to a stronger Wichita. Chung identified four challenges:

- the need to diversify Wichita's economy, which was and is heavily reliant on aerospace
- the outflow of human capital, meaning that the city and

state were losing workers, particularly skilled and educated workers
- the need to reinvigorate the city's entrepreneurial roots
- the negative perception outsiders had of Wichita[13]

All these assessments, committees, studies, and conversations converged into what Wichita State University eventually released as its very first strategic plan in April 2013. The plan outlined a new vision, mission, and seven goals to "shape the future of the university, guide decision-making, and determine resource allocations," as stated in our 2013 strategic plan.

> *Vision:* To be internationally recognized as the model for applied learning and research.
>
> *Mission:* To be an essential educational, cultural, and economic driver for Kansas and the greater public good.
>
> *Goals:* (1) Guarantee an applied learning or research experience for every student through each academic program; (2) pioneer an educational experience for all that integrates interdisciplinary curricula across the university; (3) capitalize systemically on relevant existing and emerging societal and economic trends that increase quality educational opportunities; (4) accelerate the discovery, creation, and transfer of new knowledge; (5) empower students to create a campus culture and experience that meets their changing needs; (6) be a campus that reflects—in staff, faculty, and students—the evolving diversity of society; and (7) create a new model of assessment, incentive, and reward processes to accomplish our vision and goals.[14]

Soon after releasing the strategic plan, Bardo also launched his vision for a physical place on campus, where business, industry, and academia could collaborate on the innovations and research of tomorrow. Today, this section of Wichita State is known as the Innovation Campus, and it is the physical manifestation of a ten-year transformation and expansion of the university.

Of course, the expansion of our campus didn't come without resistance. First and foremost came Wichita State's faculty, some of whom felt excluded from the expansion process, including Dr. George Dehner, an associate professor of history at Wichita State, who felt "there was a shocking lack of transparency about what the university was intending to do." As he stated, "There were, for example, some big meetings, in which the faculty were informed, 'We're building this new building' or, 'We're having this new relationship,' but there was no question about whether we thought this was the way we want the university going."[15] Bardo would explain what was happening during university town halls, but Dr. Jay Price, a professor of history, didn't feel like there were enough opportunities for faculty input. Price reflected, "There's a difference between feeling heard and feeling like you were part of the process. There was a feeling that you could vent, but it wouldn't do any good."[16]

At the same time, even those who were on board with the planning felt like it was all happening too quickly, observed Dr. Amy Drassen Ham, a medical anthropologist and clinical professor in the Department of Public Health Sciences.

She recalled, "A lot of us were deeply fatigued because it was always, 'Something new is coming, and then something else new is coming.'" She continued, "At first, there was some initial excitement, but then it started to become fatiguing because we felt like we were just in a state of constant change, change, change, change. And that was hard to keep up with. But that's the chaos that comes along with innovation."[17]

That chaos—or enthusiasm—was invigorating to Cindy Claycomb, who explained, "I liked the speed at which he [Bardo] worked. I thought it was a nice change at the university to actually move things forward that quickly. I thought he was a visionary."[18]

Change is never easy, and these were tumultuous days for Wichita State. Clearly, change was happening too fast for some people, but not fast enough for others. There were those who felt they were being excluded from the decision-making machine and others who felt the wrong people were making the decisions. In fact, from my point of view (at the time, I worked as the associate vice president for the Division of Academic Affairs), not one member from academic affairs, including the provost at the time, was included on the strategic planning steering committee that Bardo assembled.[19]

At one point, there were competing paid newspaper ads, both supporting the university—but what version of the university? One asked, "Whose university is it anyway?"[20] The other proclaimed the changes as "innovative thinking for today's realities in higher education."[21] In 2017, the administration's perceived secrecy led to a student sit-in that took over the administration building's top floor, with students demanding to hear from the president.[22] Ultimately, in a particularly contentious meeting where university police were summoned for security, WSU's Student Government Association passed a vote of "no confidence" in Bardo.[23]

Unfortunately, a perceived lack of transparency was common during John Bardo's administration, and it haunted the university for years to come—even today, to some extent. Despite publicly inviting the entire community to be included in the planning process, the perception remained that Bardo didn't invite feedback or seek wide and collective input from the university's constituency as he barreled ahead with his own agenda.

To be candid, Bardo's communication style wasn't universally embraced. He was a visionary. As such, his mind was a constant whirlwind of grand ideas. During many meetings, it seemed like he was more in the mode of thinking aloud, delivering a brain dump rather than a clear call to action. Deciphering whether his statements were mere musings for future consideration or urgent tasks for the team often posed a challenge. To navigate this, some of us developed a strategic approach: If he mentioned something once, we would take note of it but hold off on immediate action. If he mentioned it a second time, we would kick into gear, operationalizing the idea, crafting a plan, and delegating tasks. This method proved effective in bringing order to the chaos, calming the waters, and translating Bardo's vision into a tangible and actionable plan for our team.

In hindsight, the transformative era under John Bardo's leadership at Wichita State University remains a testament to the complexity of change we all experience in academia. That complexity played out in institutional decisions and in how individuals across campus felt—sometimes energized, sometimes sidelined. Dr. Jan Twomey, a professor of engineering, put it plainly: "Bardo kind of bulldozed over everyone, but someone needs to be a leader. Someone needs to say, 'This is what we're going to do. This is the direction we're going.' And as an engineering faculty, when it came to the Innovation Campus, I didn't mind that. Other people on campus were upset because they didn't have a voice in all of this. But, you know, we don't need to have a voice in everything."[24]

For his part, Bardo remained steadfast in his determination to elevate Wichita State, aiming to enhance the experience for our students and contribute positively to the broader society. In an April 2017 interview with *The Sunflower*, Wichita State's student-run newspaper, he said:

> What I'm looking at fundamentally is—are we positioned so that this university can prosper in the future? Higher education is going to change a lot, and the question is—do we get to control the changes and move ahead of them, or are we at the other end, having someone tell us we can't do those things? What we're trying to do as an administration is address how we position this university so students can benefit in the immediate and long run. We need to meet the needs of society as the means of society change.[25]

Through it all, Bardo remained committed to transforming Wichita State for the betterment of the university and the city. Lou Heldman saw this firsthand every day and was continually inspired by it. As he recalled, "[Bardo] was trying to do something very important for Wichita and very important for our students. It was exciting and a joy to be a part of. He was such a fountain of ideas." Heldman added, "It sometimes felt like being in the bunker with bombs raining down, but [Bardo] didn't feel like he needed to please everybody."[26]

Amid the shadows of this perceived opacity, one undeniable truth emerged: John Bardo's dedication to Wichita State's advancement and the broader potential of Kansas illuminated a path toward transformation.

## WHAT'S THE MAIN POINT?

Let's talk about a challenge in higher education: We are nice to each other. But ask yourself, if change is needed, is it nice to do nothing? Bardo knew he was not liked by all. I've heard it over and over: It's better to go 100 miles an hour and make a mistake than stand still and do nothing. I watched him make unpopular choices by choosing our future over status quo niceties. As university leaders, we are faced with a multitude of uncertainties; doing nothing just to be nice is not an option. Of this I am certain. How can the nice path also be the path of transformational change that serves your students, community, and partners, creating relevance for tomorrow? You may be at a crossroads. The first step to change is establishing a vision of what could be. You do not (and should not) do this alone.

## WHAT WE DID WELL

- We chose change while staying true to our vision and mission.
- We collaborated with the community through feedback and partnerships.
- We sought direction from assessments, constituent input, market demand, student voices, and research.
- We prioritized our highest contributions and obligations to Kansas.
- We had to make tough decisions and sacrifice the comfortable nest of the status quo. We had the urgency and drive to stay true to our new vision and mission.

## LESSONS LEARNED

- Vision and mission statements should be made for a purpose. Often people don't believe these are useful, but in our case, they chart our future.
- Transformational change is difficult and often painful. Though consensus is nearly impossible in a large institution, actively listening to diverse viewpoints and taking the

time to consider all voices can make the process easier—
and might even make the change palatable.

- Thought leaders may see the horizon, and it's critical to
identify who will operationalize change.

## CONSIDERATIONS FOR THE READER

If your university has it figured out and change is not needed,
skip ahead to the next chapter. If you are wrestling with forging a path to navigate the tumultuous educational landscape of
today and tomorrow, consider the following questions:

- Why do you think your institution needs change? I would
argue that the why of the change is at least as important as
the change itself.
- Who will help you activate your vision? Ideally, it would be
everyone at your institution, but that's not realistic. Strategically, who can help you build and activate your vision? Who
understands the risks of the status quo and will stand with
you as a change-bringer?
- Are you prepared for the inevitable adversity that will come
along with big change? How can you prepare yourself, your
team, and your institution to weather the storm?

....................................................................

**What to Expect in Chapter 3**

Innovation isn't just a trendy term. It's a commitment to unlocking possibilities and fostering discovery. The drive to seek knowledge is central to academia. To advance knowledge and innovation, universities must establish a robust, supportive infrastructure that fosters an environment where ideas can flourish and breakthroughs become reality. This chapter outlines the support structures we created at Wichita State to encourage, foster, and commercialize the remarkable research and innovations that have become synonymous with Shocker Nation.

# 3

## Lean Into Possibility

We also pushed the accelerator on our research—
more specifically, applied research.

There's a potential for a larger-than-life story of reinvention and renaissance at the heart of universities across our country. Diverse worldviews, a campus brimming with emerging intellects, and a network of state-of-the-art resources create living petri dishes—rich, ever-evolving cultures where innovation multiplies, ideas blossom, and breakthroughs take root.

In 2012, when John Bardo assumed the presidency at Wichita State University, he brought with him a belief that WSU could be more—more than a traditional university, more than a commuter campus, and more than our Midwestern "aw, shucks" sentiment. He challenged faculty, staff, students, and alumni to "envision being part of a university where innovation, creativity, entrepreneurship, and technology are making the future."[1] Shocker Nation accepted the challenge; today, we are a bold, audacious, problem-solving research and collaboration hub that serves the community and tackles big challenges—all while creating a more enriching and deeper educational experience for students.

Re-creating ourselves while staying true to our community and honoring our origin story has been an extraordinary and uncomfortable stunt of contortionism, but we've emerged with a level of exhilaration and hope that's only possible when we believe in the promise of tomorrow.

Before I get to WSU's innovation journey, allow me to pause on the word *innovation*. To some, it's a buzzword that is ubiquitous, overused, and even misused.

But to Wichita State, it is more than just a word. It is a frame of mind. It's a conviction we carry within us. Dr. Sheree Utash, WSU vice president of workforce development and president of WSU Tech,[2] explained: "People can say they're innovative, but tell me: What did you do lately that was innovative? It's a mindset—a growth mindset, a can-do mindset, a get-to-yes mindset."[3]

For me, Wichita State's approach to innovation is a toolbox with an endless array of implements and accessories. Through innovation, we solve problems—problems for our students, for our university, for our community, for businesses, and even for you.

Now, let's go back to how we embody innovation at Wichita State and how we built a culture around it.

Our next challenge was fostering an institutional culture of innovation—one that cultivated an environment where positive risk-taking, experimentation, and interdisciplinary collaboration not only are appreciated and encouraged but are expected and rewarded.

In his 2019 *Issues in Science and Technology* article, Bardo wrote about the Patent and Trademark Laws Amendments Act, also known as the Bayh-Dole Act, of 1980, saying it "represented a watershed event for higher education and the impact research universities could have on discovery and job growth."[4] The act allowed universities to preserve ownership of intellectual property developed through federally funded research, granting them the ability to license and commercialize their inventions.

Many universities looked at Bayh-Dole and thought it would bring a bubbling stream of revenue. That was not the case at Wichita State. However, it did open a door for the commercialization and dissemination of the research, programs, and initiatives happening on our campuses. More important, our researchers and inventors would have more control over their work, such as how it's marketed and how it's used.

In 2014, the university established WSU Ventures, the predecessor to the Office of Tech Transfer and Commercialization (TTC). Through this office, researchers at the university—including faculty, undergraduates, graduate students, and staff—work with legal counsel to navigate intellectual property and copyright procedures. This allows for the transfer of innovations from the university to the marketplace, where their true potential can be realized.

Tech transfer is not unique to Wichita State. In fact, it's a common division of most research institutions. At Wichita State, however, we saw an opportunity to use our TTC to do more than simply apply for patents. We saw potential to use our research and expertise to propel our university and community forward through the tech transfer office as we transform research into practical applications. This work cultivates an entrepreneurial spirit that launches startup companies that bring new technologies to market, spurring employment and boosting the overall prosperity for the people of our state. Rob Gerlach, the director of TTC, explained that it's all about how a university can leverage its assets to impact the community in a way that's beneficial to everyone. As he clarified, "The reason we have tech transfer and commercialization is because the people on this campus—whether they're a researcher for the National Institute for Aviation Research or fine arts faculty—are doing really amazing things that should not be locked up inside the university."[5]

For example, one unconventional and nontechnical example of WSU's tech transfer efforts is the Suspenders4Hope campaign that came out of our Student Wellness Center's Counseling and Psychological Services (CAPS) department.[6] Suspenders4Hope, as stated on the website, "is a comprehensive, strategic approach to promoting mental health wellness, preventing suicide, substance abuse, and sexual violence. We believe that hope, recovery, and resilience are possible with the right support."[7]

Mental health experts in CAPS developed the Suspenders-4Hope campaign in 2018, and it picked up steam during and after the COVID-19 pandemic when many were struggling with anxiety, isolation, and poor mental health. The campaign includes curriculum and training, strategic branding guidelines, and merchandise, as Gerlach explained: "What the CAPS team built is something that really resonates with people. We saw it, and we wanted to make sure we didn't lose it. So, we worked very closely to encourage [the CAPS team] to continue to push and go forward and build this into something more."[8]

Today, Suspenders4Hope is licensable and is widely used in diverse settings that include other universities, restaurant chains, religious organizations, health care organizations, and retail businesses.[9] Gerlach said: "It's not your typical ground-breaking technology discovery, but it's something much more approachable. We recognized that there was a mental health crisis in our community, we had a solution on our campus, and we made it widely available."[10] Whether it's translating mental health advocacy into scalable programs or launching startups through technology transfer, innovation at Wichita State takes many forms. That philosophy is also at the heart of the Master of Innovation Design (MID) program—an academic space where students shape their own paths to innovation.

The MID program—originally conceived by Anthony Vizzini, a former provost and a now-retired professor of aerospace engineering—is one example of how we are building a culture of interdisciplinary innovation. The program launched in 2015. Students in the MID program create a tailored curriculum to fit their version of innovation—whether that be a product, process, service, or idea—and take courses in core design and engineering and design-thinking-infused curriculum. Students are encouraged to take risks, experiment, and collaborate with classmates, other departments across campus, and external partners.

The success of the MID program led to the establishment of the College of Innovation and Design. We've expanded our offerings to include undergraduate courses, a minor in sustainability, and certificates in blockchain, design thinking, and interdisciplinary leadership.

While the inventions and concepts that surface from the College of Innovation and Design are remarkable on their own, the college itself stands as an archetype of inclusivity and interdisciplinary excellence.

Students with interests as varied as engineering, graphic design, psychology, and computer science converge in the College of Innovation and Design to collaborate, create, solve problems, and build the world of tomorrow. It's a unique program that speaks to the innovative nature of the university.

Of course, no bold shift comes without questions. While there were initial concerns that the Innovation Campus would be overwhelmingly engineering-heavy—dominated by labs, tech startups, and industry partnerships catering primarily to STEM disciplines—students and faculty from across the university have found ample opportunities for interdisciplinary work and research. Cheyla Clawson, an associate professor and the director of WSU's School of Performing Arts, pointed out that universities should always be a hub for interdisciplinary work: "The real world is collaborative and interdisciplinary. It's always interesting to me that university curricula and pedagogy and the systemic structure are so split apart. . . . I think that's unfortunate."[11]

As we moved forward with creating an Innovation Campus

that incorporated as many disciplines and minds as possible, we also pushed the accelerator on our research—more specifically, applied research. In the 1980s, Wichita State changed its mission to prioritize research, and we became a Research 2 (R2) Carnegie-classified research institution.[12] We also have the benefit of being in an urban environment, surrounded by a tapestry of people and businesses rich with opportunities for problem-solving.

Problem-solving has been part of Wichita State's DNA since the early days when we established the Walter H. Beech Wind Tunnel in 1948 to support the city's thriving aerospace industry.[13] Those early efforts laid the groundwork for what became our bread and butter: aviation research and development. This work helped put both Wichita State and the city itself on the map as the Air Capital of the World—serving as a crucial partner to the region's robust aerospace industry.

John Bardo had experience building industry connections during his time at Western Carolina University and went to work building those connections in Wichita by asking faculty and staff to help. The ensuing strategy to finding industry pain points, listening to needs, and identifying solutions was critical in creating an innovative culture, explained Dr. Shirley Lefever, a retired WSU provost and executive vice president: "The whole approach to having those conversations with industry and community leaders for the express purpose of meeting specific needs—that's what makes WSU and the Innovation Campus different."[14] Wichita State's sweet spot is applied research and learning that emerges from relationships

The Walter H. Beech Wind Tunnel on the Wichita State University campus conducted its first test on April 3, 1948. The wind tunnel is a closed-throat, subsonic wind tunnel that provides testing and research services for government agencies, educational institutions, and commercial companies. More than seventy-five years later, it remains in operation. Photo courtesy of WSU Libraries.

with industry partners. This is an important distinction for an urban-based institution. The university approaches applied research with the intent of working with industry partners to find a solution to a specific problem facing industry. More traditional forms of academic research are also a vital part of WSU's portfolio and are equally recognized as crucial and valuable to the university and to society at large. In fact, much of the applied research has emerged from our previously conducted basic research.

Our strategic decision to emphasize applied research stems from Wichita State's location in the largest city in the state.[15]

This setting creates an optimal environment for applied research opportunities to solve industry problems. According to Lefever, "We're at the table when they're talking about what they really need. We continue these conversations and collaboration until a solution is identified that meets their specific need. That's applied research."[16] This approach reflects an ongoing commitment to innovation and problem-solving at the heart of the university's vision and mission—even if it is different than what most people expect of a university, said Dr. John Tomblin, executive vice president for Research and Industry and Defense Programs, and executive director of WSU's NIAR: "We're tightly connected with the community's needs so we can ultimately drive the economy of Kansas. We're always on the lookout for the next problem we can solve."[17]

This problem-solving approach has garnered interest and support from the typical funders, but more so from industry, the Department of Defense, and other federal departments. Jerry Moran, a US senator who represents Kansas, has seen how Wichita State can help solve a whole host of research problems in the aerospace industry, as well as in criminal justice. Because of his seniority on various Senate committees, he regularly brings secretaries, directors and military leaders from federal departments and industry CEOs (the Departments of Commerce and Defense; the Bureau of Alcohol, Tobacco, Firearms and Explosives; the National Science Foundation; Boeing; Northrup Grumman) to Wichita State. Our experience is that leaders in Washington, DC, want to see immediate solutions to problems because their constituents want them, and we've been able to deliver on that time and time again, ultimately benefiting from millions of federal dollars directed to the university for this purpose and leading to hundreds of applied learning experiences for our students.

Today, our drive to solve problems and meet the needs of the people we serve is second nature. In 2011, before we started the push for applied research, our annual research expenditures totaled $63 million.[18] In 2024, we sat at $392 million in yearly R&D expenditures.[19] Additionally, Wichita State's R&D expenditures have nearly tripled between fiscal year 2019 and 2024, far exceeding national trends and landing north of 200 percent growth in the past five years.[20] According to recent data from the National Science Foundation:

- Wichita State is No. 1 in the nation for aerospace engineering R&D expenditures.
- Wichita State is No. 2 on the list in industry-funded engineering R&D expenditures.[21]
- Wichita State is No. 8 in the nation for overall engineering R&D expenditures.

This growth has been significantly driven by research partnerships focused on the digitization of the design and manufacturing of aircraft and other structures. Also known as digital twin, this method creates digital 3D models from physical parts and products, which allows for design modification and efficient part replacement methods, including 3D printing. This expertise has garnered partnerships with various branches of the Department of Defense and aircraft manufacturers and has led to digital transformation work with NetApp, The Smart Factory by Deloitte @ Wichita, and ATF's Crime Gun Intelligence Center of Excellence—all of which are located on our Innovation Campus.

In 2022, WSU was further recognized as the only entity in Kansas and one of twenty-one out of 529 applications nationwide awarded funding from the US Department of Commerce's Economic Development Administration Build Back Better Regional Challenge competition through the American Rescue Plan Act. Wichita State was awarded $51 million to help small businesses adopt advanced and smart manufacturing processes,[22] and Wichita State's Hub for Advanced Manufacturing Research facilitates the purpose of this grant.[23]

This milestone is part of a broader story: The Innovation Campus has paid dividends in several diverse ways beyond research. All outcomes clearly aligned with our priorities of access and affordability, feeding the talent pipeline, and increasing economic prosperity, depicted in figure 3.2. Chapter 9 offers a deeper exploration of these priorities and their role in advancing our strategic plan.

Though we celebrate our dominance in aerospace, manufacturing, and digital research, we're not as narrowly focused as that might suggest. Our researchers have created products, processes, and technologies that extend far beyond the aviation sector.

For example, in 2020, when the COVID-19 pandemic essentially shut down the world, there was widespread anxiety and uncertainty. Businesses and schools were devastated, and

| 2013 | 2014 | 2015 | 2016 | 2017 | 2018 | 2019 | 2020 | 2021 | 2022 | 2023 | 2024 |

Strategic Master Plan completed | Innovation Campus begins | Strategic Enrollment Management | I-35 corridor strategy | 2017–2024: Nearly 30 new buildings, partners and programs established

**Student applied learning earnings**

$19M $20M $20M $20M $21M $23M $24M $27M $26M $28M $35.6M $36M

**Total research grant awards**

$54M $50M $53M $74M $91M $105M $137M $165M $180M $288M $402M $411M

**Wichita State enrollment**

14,550 15,003 14,495 14,474 15,081 15,784 16,058 15,550 16,097 16,921 17,548 17,700

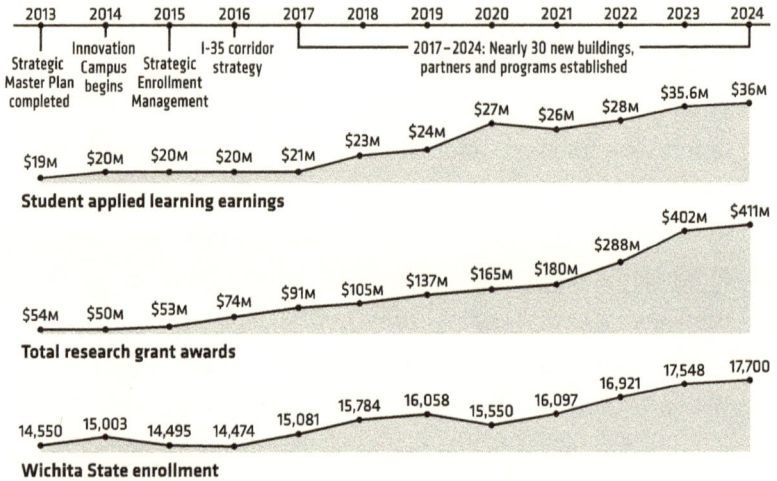

Growth of applied learning earnings, research grants and awards, and Wichita State enrollment from 2013 to 2024. For research expenditures, see page 147.

there was no clarity as to how long the lockdown would last, how bad the economy would get, or how we could effectively manage the disruption. Additionally, COVID-19 diagnostic testing was slow—sometimes taking up to a week to process one specimen. There were no fast and accessible means to test, quarantine, and treat patients. I assembled a team of experts on our campus to determine if we could build a rapid solution to sustain the local economy. Could we execute this risky project with so much depending on our success? The answer was yes.

We felt and heard the desperation of our community, and we saw an opportunity for innovation that wasn't being handled by the understandably overwhelmed medical and health care community. Product manufacturing in Wichita required in-person labor—working from home simply wasn't an option. So we pooled the collective brainpower of people from across our campus to advance a solution: engineers, medical laboratory scientists, experts in artificial intelligence, and the advanced manufacturing and automation experts from NIAR.

In October 2020, mere months after the virus's full force struck the nation, Wichita State opened the Molecular Diagnostics Laboratory (MDL), a high-throughput, high-volume, fully certified Clinical Laboratory Improvement Amendments (CLIA) testing facility that processed thousands of SARS-CoV-2 saliva-based specimens each day, with results available in less than twenty-four hours.[24]

State, industry, and educational leaders lauded the MDL as our state's best weapon in fighting the spread of the virus at the time.[25] Throughout the worst of the pandemic, the MDL processed more than half a million specimens, helping our businesses, schools, and government stay open.[26]

The MDL was possible because of the competencies available at NIAR. Our expertise in aerospace, advanced manufacturing robotics, and digital transformation converged with our research in medical laboratory sciences and health professions, allowing us to stand up a remarkable, state-of-the-art facility that helped our state find its footing in the battle against COVID-19. You might expect this type of initiative from a flagship medical school, but perhaps not from WSU, given that we don't have a medical school. Yet, our interdisciplinary approach, industry connections, and diverse expertise allowed us to step up to the challenge and make a significant impact in the fight against the pandemic and further serve the interests of Kansans.

All these tools—tech transfer, academic programming around innovation, applied research—support our innovation mindset. Wichita State University's focus on innovation represents a seismic shift in the way we teach, conduct research, learn, and grow on our campus. Ultimately, our dedication to innovation not only has transformed our campus but also exemplifies the transformative power of universities in shaping a better future for our communities.

## WHAT'S THE MAIN POINT?

Innovation is more than a buzzword. True innovation requires courage, a willingness to challenge the status quo, and the ability to embrace a different way. Coming up with new ideas is only the beginning. The real power lies in turning those ideas into positive and meaningful change. Innovation is about pushing boundaries, taking appropriate risks, and learning from failure. So, to achieve innovation, a university must be willing to invest time and resources into fostering a culture of experimentation and adaptability.

## WHAT WE DID WELL

- We created a culture of innovation, including creating degree programming and an infrastructure around innovative thinking.
- We amplified our focus on applied learning and research to solve problems for the people, businesses, and industries of Kansas.
- We tapped into our community's entrepreneurial spirit through tech transfer.

## LESSONS LEARNED

- Anyone can say they're innovative, but to truly be innovative, you must embrace positive risk-taking and build an infrastructure to support and encourage new ideas and creativity.
- I cannot emphasize how important it is to listen—really listen—to the people you serve, understand their pain points, and create solutions.

## CONSIDERATIONS FOR THE READER

- How does your institution innovate? How do you encourage and foster innovation?
- What structures and systems have you implemented to support and encourage the growth of your innovation?
- Does the culture of your institution support positive risk-taking—or even failure?

........................................................................

## What to Expect in Chapter 4

This chapter focuses on the journey and evolution of Wichita State's Innovation Campus. It also unfolds a more universal narrative about innovative change and the creative utilization of assets. While you explore this chapter, consider the untapped resources within your own institution. You likely have assets—whether an underutilized building, uninspired classroom space, or a vacant plot of land—that are just waiting to help you make a transformative impact.

# 4

## Manifest the Vision

It was a shock to see how rapidly everything happened.

Since its founding in 1895, Wichita State has embraced possibility. The visionary foresight to establish a college in a city that was just starting to lay down its roots was a risky venture indeed. Over the decades, that same spirit of boldness endured and evolved with the needs of the city and its people. By 2014, Wichita State leaders were looking at a new possibility in the form of campus expansion: the Innovation Campus.

To understand how the Innovation Campus came to be the model of industry and academic partnerships that it is today,[1] we must go way back to 1967, when the Wichita State Board of Trustees purchased Crestview Country Club's golf course, a 120-acre plot contiguous to campus, for future campus expansion.[2] Renamed as Braeburn Golf Course, for forty-five years, it remained a neatly manicured golf course enjoyed by our golf team and wider community.

In 2014, President John Bardo announced that he had other plans for the golf course: a cutting-edge research park to support industry through advanced research capabilities and students with applied learning and research opportunities.[3]

This vision, the Innovation Campus, would be a destination spot for the community to include apartments, retail establishments, restaurants, and—of course—buildings where companies could create and compete. But before all that happened, a few pieces of the puzzle needed to be put into place.

The first task was to physically locate students at the front and center of our main campus. As part of the vision to change the perception of WSU from that of a commuter campus and improve the student-life experience, the university wanted to bring student housing into the heart of the main campus. This meant razing two dilapidated structures on the outskirts of campus—the Wheatshocker Apartments and the Fairmount Towers residence hall—and replacing them with updated modern facilities that met the demands of students. In 2014, WSU opened Shocker Hall, a brand-new on-campus home for first-year students that included all the modern accoutrements students could want: a dining hall with a robust menu, a coffee and snack shop, a full kitchen and laundry room on every floor, Foosball, a pool table, and dorm rooms that could accommodate anywhere from one to four students. Best of all, it was built just steps from the student union, the Shocker basketball and volleyball arena, and many academic buildings. This shift toward a more traditional on-campus experience was highlighted by Bardo during the grand opening of Shocker Hall in 2014, at which he stated, "We are celebrating a change in the life of the university associated with increasing the quality of student experience . . . we are changing their experience to offer them the opportunity to get to know each other, work

Built in 2014, Shocker Hall is the oldest of Wichita State's residence
halls. The five-story building houses about eight hundred of Wichita
State's first-year students. It is located near the center of campus
and includes private and shared rooms with modern amenities. The
building also houses the Dorothy and Bill Cohen Honors College and the
four-hundred-seat Shocker Dining Hall.

together and to collaborate—to enjoy each other and be part
of a major, emerging national research university."[4] The university's improved on-campus living experience kept going
from there, with two more student housing facilities built since
then—The Flats and The Suites—that offer an apartment, in-
dependent style of living.

The next step was to make room for the intended research
park. In November 2014, it was announced that Braeburn Golf
Course would close to make way for the Innovation Campus.[5]
As you can imagine, some golfers did not appreciate being displaced, but community support for the plan to invigorate the
university and the city started early, with Bob Lutz, a former
sports editor for *The Wichita Eagle* newspaper, weighing in:

"This is a good thing for Wichita State. Even the most rabid golfer has to sign off on a plan that could help Wichita become more than just aerospace, agriculture and oil."[6]

But along with community support came internal push-back. Some faculty felt excluded from decisions about which companies would be a good fit for the university. Dr. Bayram Yildirim, an industrial engineering professor who was the Faculty Senate president from 2016 to 2017, championed the idea that faculty must be involved in providing feedback on potential tenants to ensure that the Innovation Campus would serve as a hub to support WSU's vision, mission, and strategic priorities. As a result, President Bardo supported the faculty's request to be more involved with the decision-making process.

It all just happened so fast, according to history professor Dr. Jay Price. He explained, "For a lot of the faculty, they simply knew the golf course as the golf course. A lot of us knew that the golf course was overflow space and was always intended to be so; but it was a shock to see how rapidly everything happened. I still remember when there was this beautiful, massive tree there; and then the next day, it was on its side and dying. It was just an unsettling sight."[7]

There was still a great amount of strong support for Bardo and an invigorating excitement about the transformation happening at the northeast corner of Wichita State, even if there was no consensus on how that transformation was playing out, said Dr. Gery Markova, a professor and the director of Wichita State's hospitality and master's of human resource management programs. As Markova put it, "We never know if a decision is good until we see it in implementation, and whether he did it the right way or not, he was an implementer."[8]

Dr. Mark Vermillion, chair of WSU's Department of Sport Management, liked the idea of the Innovation Campus, even if he couldn't quite picture the end product. As he said, "A college campus should always be about evolution and reinvention, and that's what the Innovation Campus was all about."[9]

This evolution and reinvention involved conversations with many potential new business partners—businesses that weren't ready to have their names mentioned before contracts were signed. So, as you can imagine, complaints that the administration wasn't communicating or being transparent enough got louder and louder. Faculty particularly valued shared governance. According to *The Sunflower*, the student newspaper, in March 2017 the Faculty Senate sent a letter to Bardo listing its constituency's concerns, stating that "the idea of shared governance is a concept that has fallen into disrepair under the current administration."[10] The letter also noted that "input from faculty is 'often nonexistent' . . . superficial at best and patronizing at worst."[11] While Bardo's intent wasn't malicious, he was on a mission; his position was about finding people who were willing to take risks and make big changes, said Andy Schlapp, vice president of strategy and government relations at Wichita State. "Bardo focused on people who were willing to take the first step. This caused some resentment, and people said that those people who were willing to take that first step were in the inner circle."[12]

The rub among some internal and external stakeholders

was a perceived lack of transparency specifically in the way the Innovation Campus was being built—a process where private developers gained a ground lease from WSU for what some believed was below market value. The developer would then build the facilities and lease them to partners on the Innovation Campus. This approach, although common elsewhere, had not happened before at Wichita State. Some community members and faculty believed this private development model—where a developer leases university land, constructs facilities, retains lease revenue, and assumes financial risk—should not be the purpose of a public institution. It was advantageous to WSU, however, as the financing for a new research park would never be available through state funding to higher education. In addition, the Innovation Campus partners were obligated to employ our students with applied learning experiences, fulfilling one of the original purposes of the Innovation Campus—a new model for applied learning and research curriculum that would prepare students for future careers while solving our community talent pipeline needs.

Adding to the complexity of this evolution was the controversy surrounding The Wonder School, a private pre-K through grade 12 school built on WSU's campus. The school, which opened in 2018 and has since moved to an off-campus location, sparked a heated debate on campus and in the community. Critics had perceptions about the exclusivity of the school. Many questioned whether it was appropriate for a public university to host such a private institution, especially one that would cater to a select, high-income demographic. Some staff and faculty were upset that they had little to no knowledge that it was opening on campus. Supporters, however, viewed it as a valuable innovation experiment, aligning with WSU's broader mission of educational and community transformation.[13] This tension underscored the university's ongoing challenge of balancing the pursuit of innovative partnerships with the need to ensure that such collaborations benefit a broad spectrum of the community.

Despite the resistance, Bardo's administration went full steam ahead. The team began working on building infrastructure on the Innovation Campus, and the Experiential Engineering Building opened in 2017.[14] It's a 143,000-square-foot, three-story facility with twenty-five labs, a spacious open-concept lobby, and a makerspace where anyone can obtain membership to access sophisticated equipment and expert training for prototyping, projects, or hobbies. Membership is open to the public and is free for full-time students. After Dr. Bardo's death in 2019, the building was renamed the John Bardo Center.[15]

Almost simultaneously with the opening of the Experiential Engineering Building, the Innovation Campus attracted its first big resident: Airbus Americas, an aerospace firm headquartered in France that designs and manufactures commercial and military aircraft. Airbus, which represented hundreds of jobs in Wichita,[16] was on the verge of leaving the area, which would have devastated the city's engineering community, according to John Tomblin, executive vice president for Research and Industry and Defense Programs and executive director of NIAR.[17]

After extensive talks and planning, Airbus decided it liked what it saw of the Innovation Campus's grand plan and announced in 2015 that the company would remain in the Wichita area and locate its US engineering headquarters on WSU's Innovation Campus. As Bardo said during the press conference to announce the news, the commitment by Airbus represented a massive step forward for our students, the state of Kansas, and the Innovation Campus: "This secures WSU's future as a global center of engineering and will encourage other world-class firms to locate on our campus."[18] He was right. Since 2015, several more aerospace and business giants have found homes on the Innovation Campus, including Spirit AeroSystems, Textron Aviation, NetApp, Hexagon, Deloitte, and Dassault Systèmes, to name a few. See image on page 17 for more detailed information on WSU's Innovation Campus partners.

It wasn't long before the community noticed that Wichita State University was on the precipice of something extraordinary—and not just for the aerospace industry. Even those working closely in the aerospace sphere, like Tracee Friess, the associate vice president of strategic communications and marketing for WSU's Industry and Defense Programs, were excited to see the university branch out. As Friess stated:

When we attracted Dassault Systèmes, Hexagon, and Airbus—three global partners—I thought, "OK, maybe we can do this." But for me, it was the Law Enforcement Training Center, because that was a facility that Wichita had needed for a very long time, and no one could agree on where to do it or how to do it. That was the turning point for me because it was a completely different sector. It was not engineering-related. It was criminal justice. That's another very strong program at Wichita State, and having the center here on the Innovation Campus just makes it even stronger.[19]

The integration of the Law Enforcement Training Center (LETC) within the Innovation Campus was a natural and strategic alignment. It engaged non-engineering students and faculty, who often voiced frustration at feeling left out of the vision, growth, and development of the Innovation Campus. This was particularly important for members of the Fairmount College of Liberal Arts and Sciences, which houses the nation's second-oldest criminal justice program.[20]

Serendipitously, the Wichita and Sedgwick County law enforcement communities had been searching for a new home for the LETC, which previously had been housed in a sixty-year-old former elementary school. The Innovation Campus was a significant step up not only from a location standpoint but also for local law enforcement's future, as Dr. John Tomblin explained: "We started growing the workforce differently for Airbus and Dassault Systèmes and some of our other partners, and we wanted to take what we've done and extend it beyond engineering. We were going to extend this to criminal justice and produce the future workforce for our law enforcement officers."[21] Currently, the LETC is home base for training and education for the law enforcement communities in Wichita, Sedgwick County, and our own Wichita State

Police Department. Moreover, the center attracts personnel from across the state for specialized training and professional development. And WSU's School of Criminal Justice is located within the LETC building, providing students and faculty with a unique chance to engage with the law enforcement community as part of their everyday environment.

In 2019, the LETC established the Crime Gun Intelligence Center, which uses state-of-the-art technology to compare and analyze shell casings collected at crime scenes.[22] This is significant in that the work and research done through the Crime Gun Intelligence Center caught the attention of the Bureau of Alcohol, Tobacco, Firearms and Explosives (ATF), which is one of the newest residents of our Innovation Campus. The ATF brought with it the Crime Gun Intelligence Center of Excellence and the National Integrated Ballistic Information Network, "the only national network that allows for the 3D imaging and comparison of ballistic evidence recovered from crime scenes."[23]

We've also built infrastructure within the Innovation Campus that supports research and entrepreneurship, and this is what has continued to attract business partnerships. This infrastructure includes the Digital Research and Transformation Hub, home to WSU's National Institute for Research and Digital Transformation; the Jerry Moran Center, home to the Advanced Virtual Engineering and Testing Labs; and the Hub for Advanced Manufacturing Research. Our faculty, staff, and industry partners use these facilities to drive innovation and prepare students for emerging technologies and future associated jobs.

Another critical part of Wichita State's ongoing transformation was building Wayne and Kay Woolsey Hall, home of the W. Frank Barton School of Business—the first fully academic building on the Innovation Campus and the first new academic building on the main campus in more than thirty years. Woolsey Hall, which opened its doors in 2022, represents the university's commitment to creating spaces that blend academics, research, and industry partnerships in an innovative environment.

Upon being named dean of the Barton Business School in 2019, Dr. Larisa Genin was responsible for shaping and guiding the vision of Woolsey Hall. As she later stated in an interview, "When I arrived, I was informed that this space had been allocated for the Barton School, and I was tasked with leading the visioning, construction, and implementation. After consulting with stakeholders, I realized we weren't just building a building. We were creating a destination."[24]

Woolsey Hall was designed to be a magnet that attracts students as well as corporate partners and the community. Its physical layout, from the architecture to the landscaping and art, was designed to reflect the vision for the Barton School. The goal was to position the Barton School as one of the top business schools in the nation, creating a hub for learning, innovation, and collaboration.

One of the most striking features of Woolsey Hall is the

Wayne and Kay Woolsey Hall, a $60 million, 125,000-square-foot academic building on Wichita State University's Innovation Campus, is the home of the W. Frank Barton School of Business.

Promise Bridge, which physically connects Wichita State's main campus with its Innovation Campus. Genin said it was designed to symbolize the connections among academics, research, and industry: "The Promise Bridge is shaped like a letter Y to represent the connection between these key elements. Everything we did was carefully curated to align with our vision for the Barton School, blending academics with a corporate and hospitality flair."[25]

Since opening, Woolsey Hall has become a central hub for students, corporate partners, and the Wichita community. The space has hosted strategic retreats for organizations such as Cargill and Textron Aviation, as well as numerous events for nonprofits and K-12 students. The building's atmosphere of innovation has made it a sought-after destination for groups across industries.

Dean Genin emphasized that the goal was to create an environment that felt welcoming for all: "We wanted Woolsey Hall to feel like a home away from home, especially for our first-generation students and those coming from diverse backgrounds. One student told me that the building felt like a 'big bear hug,' which is exactly the warmth and community we were aiming to create."[26]

But it's not all work on the Innovation Campus. We also designed the campus as a place to "learn, work, live, and play."[27] It's a microcosm with several restaurants, a hotel, a YMCA, and retail establishments.

The number and diversity of partners matter—but even more important is how we manage those relationships. Everyone who joins our Innovation Campus does so knowing it must be a two-way commitment. It's not just a transactional relationship where we lease land at a great value, according to Zach Gearhart, Wichita State's chief of staff, who explained: "We focus on a relationship that is ongoing for the benefit of our students, our researchers, and our society, and I think that's what is exceptional."[28] In every sense, the Innovation Campus is a win-win-win: It's a win for thousands of our students who work in paid applied learning and research positions with our partners (I'll address this further in chapter 7). It's a win for the companies that benefit from the research partnerships and student workers who become part of the talent pipeline.

And it's a win for the people of our city, state, and region who benefit from the full-time employment opportunities, entrepreneurial cultivation, increasing prosperity, and burgeoning economic diversity on the Innovation Campus.

Today, Wichita State University's Innovation Campus stands as a tangible manifestation of the transformative journey that has redefined how we approach education, research, partnerships, and our connection to the people and businesses of Kansas.

## WHAT'S THE MAIN POINT?

The land where the Innovation Campus started was a perfectly lovely golf course: eighteen holes of well-maintained and lush greenery. But it wasn't part of how we needed to evolve as an institution. It didn't advance our mission or vision, and it did very little to enhance the student experience beyond the athletes on the golf team. Transitioning to the Innovation Campus provided the tangible demonstration of innovation that we were cultivating throughout campus. It elevated our presence in the community, and it invited business and industry to take a seat at the table where big ideas were happening.

## WHAT WE DID WELL

- We recognized that the 120-acre plot of land on the northeast corner of campus had potential beyond being a golf course.

- We put a focus on research that drives innovation and creates solutions.
- We built a community and entrepreneurial infrastructure around innovation and applied learning.

## LESSONS LEARNED

While John Bardo was an incredible innovator and visionary, his communication style—or lack thereof—left many in the campus community feeling alienated and excluded from both the university's future and the process of shaping it. This is something I always have in the back of my mind, making sure people are informed and have access to me.

## PROXIMITY IS A PRIORITY

We had partnerships with business and industry prior to building the Innovation Campus. In fact, some of our partnerships go back decades. But having those partners on campus, working closely with students and faculty daily, makes a significant difference in how we engage with them.

## CONSIDERATIONS FOR THE READER

- While not every institution is attached to an underutilized swath of land like Wichita State was, what assets do you have that could manifest your mission, help grow your influence in your community, or create stronger programming for your students?
- If you're considering a physical change, what kind of resources do you have to transform the space, maintain it, and eventually scale up? For Wichita State, developers assumed responsibility for building and leasing spaces and buildings on the Innovation Campus. Consider whether that model might work for you or if your project would instead be entirely institutionally funded.

........................................................................

**What to Expect in Chapter 5**

One of the mistakes university leaders often make is trying to fit their institution into a traditional higher education model; in our case, we simply do not fit that mold. So, we created our own model, one in which we're helping to solve community problems through our expertise. In the process, we're providing students with cutting-edge, impactful, and transferable experiences. This approach has set us apart, and that's exactly what today's higher education leaders must do: embrace what makes their institutions distinct. In a landscape where students have endless options, success comes not from following the crowd but from understanding your strengths, knowing who you serve, and staying committed to your mission.

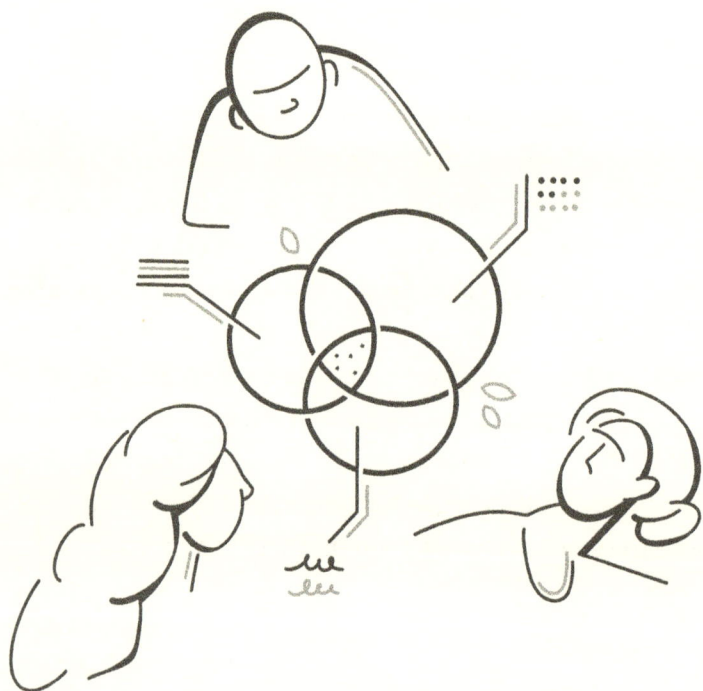

# 5

## Embrace Your Identity

We're not afraid of hard work. . . . Whether it involves harvesting
wheat . . . or cultivating a culture centered around innovation . . .
we roll up our sleeves and get the job done.

First-time visitors to Wichita might be surprised to find
themselves amid a sophisticated metropolis of business and industry giants, a thriving arts scene, ample casual
and fine dining spots, and big-name and boutique shopping
experiences.

If you've never been here, let me dispel a few myths:

- Wichita State is not in the middle of a prairie or a cornfield.
- In my more than thirty years of living here, I've never seen
  a cattle drive through downtown.
- Tornadoes are rare.
- We drive cars to work—not horses or buggies.

While we celebrate our city and the state's deep farming
and ranching roots, today's Wichita is much more connected
to microbreweries and advanced manufacturing than to the
Chisholm Trail or chuckwagons.

Here are a few Wichita factoids that might surprise you:

- We are the largest city,[1] and one of the most diverse, in Kansas.[2]
- The Wichita metro area has the highest concentration of aerospace manufacturing employment in the nation.[3]
- Wichita is home to more than 450 companies in the aerospace manufacturing supply chain that design and build general aviation, commercial, and defense products.[4]
- Zillow ranked Wichita as the most affordable housing market for first-time buyers in 2022.[5]
- According to the Brookings Institution, Wichita ranks first in the nation for the ratio of manufacturing jobs in major metropolitan areas in the United States and is the No. 3 US metropolitan area for advanced industry clusters.[6]
- The Dwight D. Eisenhower National Airport is served by most of the major airlines.[7]
- We see about 225 sunny days a year.[8]
- Wichita sits at the junction of several major highways, notably I-35 going north and south. It is also just ninety miles south of I-70 going east and west.
- In 2023, WalletHub ranked Wichita as one of the top summer travel destinations.[9]

## A QUICK HISTORY LESSON

Wichita was founded in 1868 and incorporated in 1870.[10] And after a handful of years as a rough-and-tumble trading post

In August 1927, seventeen men stand on a wing of a prototype model of a Cessna cabin monoplane. The photo was taken to demonstrate the strength of the airplane without struts to support the wings. Photo courtesy of WSU Libraries.

and cattle town, Wichita rose to prominence as an economic and commercial hub, quickly establishing a board of trade and an early version of a chamber of commerce.[11]

In 1916, the city earned its wings, so to speak, as the Air Capital of the World, when Clyde Cessna signed a contract to begin manufacturing airplanes.[12] Today, about 35 percent of all US-built planes and parts are manufactured in Kansas,[13] by companies like Spirit AeroSystems (reacquired by Boeing), Beechcraft and Cessna (both Textron Aviation companies), and Bombardier—all with deep roots and still growing in Wichita.

As our city gained traction in aviation manufacturing and

engineering, Wichita's burgeoning entrepreneurial spirit took hold and branched out into diverse industries. A few of the companies founded in Wichita include The Coleman Company, Koch Industries, Pizza Hut (started by two WSU students), Vornado, Rent-A-Center, Residence Inn, Candlewood Hotels, Freddy's Frozen Custard, and White Castle.

However, somewhere along the way, our city started to lose touch with our entrepreneurial roots. Fewer startups and investments in our community, along with stagnant population growth, were setting up Wichita for a steep decline and a talent exodus. In a report about Wichita, the economist James Chung had a clear vision for the city's entrepreneurial future: "Getting this population back will take more than a focus on entrepreneurial infrastructure like incubators and workspaces. It takes creating a culture that encourages investment and inspires innovation in the entrepreneurs already here and the ones to come."[14] As the city sought ways to revitalize itself and rekindle that pioneering spirit of entrepreneurship, Wichita State University was reimagining its own potential, striving to redefine and reconnect to our identity while reshaping the future of higher education. It was clear that the success of the city and that of the university were intertwined. They always had been. And perhaps—over the years, as the university became more insular and siloed in its academic endeavors—the synergy between the city and university had ebbed.

We wanted to bolster that bond with the people and businesses of our city, help Wichita reclaim our innovative legacy, and embrace our history en route to finding ourselves.

Discovery required honesty about who we are versus who we were trying to be.

Wichita State, originally Fairmount College, was envisioned to be the Vassar of the West.[15] The neighboring streets were—and still are—named after prominent East Coast schools: Yale, Holyoke, Vassar, and Harvard, to name a few.

That is how we started, but it's not who we are.

The East Coast university model, known for its exclusivity and prestige, doesn't translate effectively to Wichita State University—nor does it, I might argue, to most Midwestern universities. We have a distinct culture, we're not afraid to get our hands dirty, and we serve a diverse community of students.

While more traditional universities might prioritize exclusivity and prestige, Wichita State emphasizes community and accessibility. Instead of catering to a select few, Wichita State is committed to serving a diverse student population, ensuring that education is within reach for individuals of all ages, classes, backgrounds, and cultures.

We are a community of hardworking pioneers and entrepreneurs who aren't afraid of taking positive risks.

As a community, we're known as Shocker Nation. As mentioned earlier, the name Shocker goes back to the earliest days of our history when our football players would earn money for tuition by harvesting wheat—also known as shocking wheat. During the 1904 season, a football manager came up with the team's name, Wheat Shockers, to promote an upcoming game, but it wasn't until 1948 that the mascot was made official.[16] Eventually, the name was shortened to Shockers and

A student is seen shocking—or harvesting—wheat. Tradition has it that in 1904, football manager and student R. J. Kirk needed a name for the team to advertise Fairmount's upcoming game, and he came up with the name Wheatshockers because many Fairmount football players earned tuition and board shocking wheat during the summer harvests. Photo courtesy of WSU Libraries.

our mascot was named WuShock (WU, being an abbreviation for Wichita University, our name before we entered the state higher education system).[17] And, for those of you unfamiliar with our mascot, WuShock is "a big, bad, muscle-bound bundle of wheat."[18]

WuShock symbolizes our willingness to embrace hard work and diligence without hesitation. Whether work involves harvesting wheat in the fields or cultivating innovation to forge a brighter future, we readily roll up our sleeves and get the job done. So, we went to work on rebuilding and redefining our relationship with our city by listening to the people and businesses we serve and leveraging our university as an engine for the greater public good.

Our first task was to look at our students and community to understand who we currently serve, who we should serve better, and how to identify problems and pain points. In other words, we wanted to ensure we created an environment that supported the needs of our community. The sentiment at the time—as Lou Heldman, now retired vice president for the Office of Strategic Communications under President Bardo, explained—was that the city and university needed to thrive together: "That was the basis of everything that Bardo did."[19]

One example of that shared progress was the decision to support Airbus's relocation from downtown Wichita to the Innovation Campus—an important step in retaining the city's engineering base and strengthening the university's industry partnerships. While this move was a major win for both Wichita State and the region's economy, it also left a significant vacancy downtown. In response, Bardo made the intentional choice to backfill that space with health sciences programming, helping to maintain momentum in the city center and contributing to Wichita's broader growth in the biomedical sector.[20]

Now, as I mentioned previously, Bardo had been with the university briefly in the 1970s as a professor of sociology, but he'd been gone a long time and, as Zach Gearhart explained, needed to reacquaint himself with Wichita by absorbing as much information as possible: "His first year here, all he did was listen so that he could understand where the community was. He kind of understood the core of our DNA, but he wanted a deeper understanding of the community's expectations and challenges. What did businesses need? What do the city and state need from us? What is it truly going to take to grow as an institution and community?"[21] And as Bardo delved into those meaningful conversations, a profound understanding emerged regarding Wichita State's potential to reshape the state's dynamics, solidifying its role as an anchor institution for Wichita. From the onset, he emphasized to both the campus and the wider community that Wichita State's fundamental purpose is to positively transform lives, as he wrote in a 2018 essay titled "Renewing Wichita's Promise: The University, the City, the Region and Economic Development": "WSU has unique historical links to this region, long-standing programs in critical technical areas, and a renewed commitment to serving the people of the state. Because of this, WSU is positioned to benefit the local community through the research of its faculty and the education of its students, who become contributors to the local economy and the Wichita area community upon graduation."[22]

Through the act of listening—really listening—we discovered what made Wichita State distinctive. It wasn't a single program or facility but a way of thinking: leveraging research and academic expertise to respond to real-world needs. What emerged from those conversations was a deepened sense of purpose—one rooted in tackling talent gaps, fueling economic growth, and addressing community challenges head-on. Our

niche wasn't something we created; it was something we un-
covered through engagement, reflection, and the willingness
to show up for our city and state.

In 2016, Dr. Shirley Lefever, who was then the dean of the
College of Applied Studies (which houses the School of Education) and now is a retired provost of the university, was
working to build those community connections.

As Lefever met with superintendents, principals, and ed-
ucators, she heard repeatedly that they wanted help in addressing the teacher shortage for their respective districts. As
she recalled, "At first, like any relationship, you have to get to
know somebody, and as you do, you build trust. I did not go
into the conversation or relationship to fix anything. Instead, I
asked for their ideas. I would say, 'If you could build a degree
program to meet your workforce needs, what would it look
like?'"[23] Through those conversations and the trust-building
process, Lefever heard increasing alarm about the teacher
shortage, particularly in elementary and special education areas. She and her team talked with stakeholders about how the
university could increase the flow of teachers into the talent
pipeline—not just in Wichita but across the state.

Lefever recognized that we already had a talent pool, people
who were already living in the communities and working in
school settings but were not licensed teachers. This dedicated
and knowledgeable talent pool consisted of paraeducators.
From these conversations, the college developed a fully online
teacher preparation program to allow paraeducators to remain
in their current positions in their home community while

earning a teaching degree and licensure as an early childhood or elementary educator. Most important, as they matriculated through the program and met certain criteria, paraeducators who were students in the Teacher Apprentice Program (TAP) could become teachers of record in their final year and earn a full teacher salary. For many of these individuals, this was an opportunity they had never imagined because they could not afford to quit their full-time paraeducator jobs to pursue a degree, leaving them stuck in a lower-paying job. Raising their income was important to their own family's economic prosperity and to the economic prosperity of their communities.

In 2017, Wichita State launched the Teacher Apprentice Program,[24] built on the idea of an inverted curriculum. This approach delivers key professional courses at the start of the program to quickly enhance the skills of paraeducators and boost their classroom effectiveness from the beginning of their academic journey. By starting with professional courses and building on their strengths, students were more confident as they matriculated through the program. Knowing many of these students faced challenges in previous attempts at higher education, the goal of the program was for students to first experience heightened success in their jobs, followed by building resilience and confidence to complete courses they might not have succeeded at previously. As explained by Jill Wood, coordinator of WSU's TAP, "If our students had to quit their jobs for a semester to student teach, it would drastically affect their income, and the school district would lose a valuable employee. By allowing students to use the experience and knowledge they gain in the classroom on a daily basis as credit for their internship courses, it benefits everyone."[25] The first cohort of TAP had approximately ninety students in fall 2017. Just seven years later, in fall 2024, enrollment was at nearly seven hundred students and climbing, a clear indication of the level of demand for this program, said Sean Hudspeth, the chief human resources officer for Wichita Public Schools: "TAP is a vital source of recruiting and retention for Wichita Public Schools. We value the quality and services that come from our partnership with WSU in order to hire talented teaching professionals across our district. The paras that transition to teaching through this program excel, as they have mastered skills in the classroom early in their career."[26]

Graduates of the program can transition from earning an hourly wage to a full-time teaching salary with benefits—a difference TAP graduate Sara Eubank felt immediately. She recalled: "The TAP program allowed me to connect my education requirements to my job in the education system. After graduating from the program, I have had the opportunity to provide my family with extras that were not in the budget before I earned my degree in elementary education."[27] Over the years, the number of school districts employing TAP students and graduates has continued to grow, from twenty in the first year to over two hundred in 2023.[28] The program has been extremely successful—so much so that the Kansas Department of Education has adopted Wichita State's TAP as a statewide model that other universities can implement through their own education programs.[29]

Some other examples of how we work to solve problems come to us through Wichita State's National Institute for Aviation Research (NIAR). While NIAR has hundreds of projects happening at any given moment, I want to focus on two: Digital Twin and NIAR MRO, which includes Maintenance Repair and Overhaul (MRO), Environmental Test, and Flight Test Certification programs.

Through the Digital Twin program, NIAR takes legacy military airplanes and ground vehicles—some of them built as far back as the 1950s—and brings them into the digital age by disassembling them piece by piece, cleaning the pieces, scanning them, and digitally reassembling them. Through this technology, technicians who work on vehicles and aircraft can complete routine maintenance more efficiently and even virtually fit test replacement part designs by referring to the digital twin created at Wichita State.[30]

Similarly, Wichita State's MRO—a unique endeavor for a university—also brings new life to aging and underutilized aircraft. One such program has its roots in the COVID-19 pandemic. As international travel slowed and online purchasing increased, the need for more passenger aircraft decreased while the need for cargo aircraft grew. Through this program, passenger aircraft such as Boeing 777 and Airbus 321 planes are converted into freighter planes, repurposing them for a new life.[31]

We are also addressing emergency response needs through the conversion of Boeing 737s into ocean oil disbursement planes and McDonnell Douglas MD-80 aircraft to fight wildfires.

These Wichita State NIAR programs have employed hundreds of students in applied learning positions as well as full-time engineers, scientists, and technicians. We have also solved problems for the military and industry and have created economic synergy within the city of Wichita, where the work is being performed.

Other examples of how Wichita State's researchers are using their expertise and resources to solve problems include a smartphone app for those with visual impairments to read and follow the flow of graphic novels and comic books,[32] a program to educate thousands of forcibly displaced refugee children and their parents,[33] a project to mitigate the environmental impact of road salt,[34] and an innovative scaffolding system to treat burn wounds.[35] This is simply the kind of work Shockers do, according to Dr. Lefever, who stated, "I think the community sees us as being more relevant, and they see themselves as having an open invitation to have conversations with our people. I think anybody or any business—small or large—would feel comfortable calling us up and, instead of us telling them what they should be focusing on, they say, 'Hey, I've got this problem. Is there anybody that can work with me on it?'"[36]

As the university's academic and community focus took a more confident shape, we looked at other ways we could strategically broaden our sphere of influence.

The university embarked on a self-assessment and peer analysis to better align our strategic direction with our urban research university identity. During this time, the university analyzed its position among peer institutions. In July 2017, the university accepted an invitation to transition from the Missouri Valley Conference to the American Athletic Conference, known as The American. This pivotal decision emerged after a two-year evaluation process to assess how WSU athletics was intended to serve as a catalyst for enrollment expansion and bolster the university's standing as a beacon of academic and research excellence.

Speaking at a press conference, President Bardo articulated the rationale behind this landmark shift: "It became clear to us that The American offered the best combination of universities that share our academic and cultural values and research focus. The University of Tulsa, Southern Methodist University (in Dallas), and the University of Houston are located in areas of Oklahoma and Texas that make up part of the prime areas where we want to recruit students."[37] Southern Methodist University and the University of Houston have both left the American Athletic Conference and joined other athletic conferences, but they have been replaced by the University North Texas (near Dallas) and Rice University in Houston.

The decision to join The American, the shift in our research focus, and a renewed emphasis on community—no doubt these were seismic shifts in Wichita State's trajectory. But to many in Shocker Nation, it was like coming home. No longer were we attempting to emulate the East Coast schools that WSU's founders aspired us to be. Instead, we learned that our pathway to excellence was paved with the pioneering spirit of the people we serve.

## WHAT'S THE MAIN POINT?

Wichita State is not—and does not want to be—an elite private East Coast or flagship institution. We eschewed the traditional model of higher education and forged our own path. We looked at what makes Wichita State great and moved forward with plans to amplify our areas of exceptionality to focus on solving problems for our students, our community, and our state.

## WHAT WE DID WELL

- We made an intentional effort to embrace our city's entrepreneurial roots and reconnect with the pioneering spirit that made us the Air Capital of the World.
- We embraced discomfort as a necessary ingredient for progress, knowing that meaningful change rarely feels easy at the start.
- We translated big-picture vision into concrete action—anchoring our strategy in transparency, accountability, and momentum.

## LESSONS LEARNED

- As universities nationwide are struggling to remain relevant, it's vital that university leaders take inventory of who they serve and how we serve them.
- We built relationships and created solutions through our applied learning and applied research.

## CONSIDERATIONS FOR THE READER

- Do you know who you are as an institution? Are you trying to be something counter to your values? Do you know who or what your community needs you to be? If not, this is where you start. If you put aside the expectations of what you think you ought to be, what do you do best?
- Who are your constituents, and how do you serve each of them?
- How can you make a real difference for your constituents? That might be research, community projects, or development of a curriculum to meet the demands of business.

........................................................................

### What to Expect in Chapter 6

The past decade has been pivotal for higher education, as universities have grappled with evolving expectations, shifting public sentiments, and a call for institutions to go beyond traditional roles and actively contribute to societal needs. The call for accountability and community engagement echoes a sentiment felt across higher education globally. Wichita State, as a public institution accountable to the people of our state, respects the shifting landscape and has embraced the opportunity to take a hard look at who we serve and how we serve them.

# 6

## Who Do You Serve?

It's a fight between what higher ed wanted to be and what
the public was asking higher ed to be.

Higher education is at a crossroads. As public expectations shift and constant changes in Washington, DC, create uncertainty, universities are feeling the impact where it hurts most: shrinking funding and declining enrollment.[1] The message is clear: Institutions must evolve to meet these changing demands or risk becoming irrelevant in an increasingly competitive landscape.

People are no longer willing to spend their time and money to pursue intellectual curiosity in the ivory towers of higher education. Universities, particularly public universities, are expected to be accountable contributors to their communities. That sentiment is clear, explained Andy Schlapp, vice president of strategy and government relations: "It's a fight between what higher education wanted to be and what the public was asking higher education to be."[2] The public was shouting to higher education leaders that job creation was needed, along with economic stability and a thriving community. Many leaders in higher education, however, gave a chagrined shrug and said, "It's not really what we do here." Gaining an education for the sake of learning and absorption of knowledge is fantastic, says Dr. Gery Markova, a professor and chair of Wichita State's Department of Management, "but at the end of the day, you have to be able to do something that contributes to society."[3] So rather than enduring enrollment declines, crossing our fingers, and hoping for the best, we adapted.

Building on the ideas his predecessors Eugene Hughes and Donald Beggs, who envisioned WSU as a metropolitan or urban-serving university, Bardo wanted to learn what some of the problems were that Wichita State could help solve.

In Bardo's vision, a university—particularly a public university—should connect with the community in a deep and meaningful way, not just as a place where community members went to pursue a degree but a place where academia, business, and industry could collaborate to develop solutions to the problems of today and build the innovations of tomorrow.

One of the biggest problems highlighted in the Chung Report—and one that President Bardo strongly echoed—was the out-migration of talent from Kansas. Far too many Kansans were taking their talent, earning potential, and often their Wichita State diploma and leaving the state—at an alarming rate. In the early 1900s, Kansas was home to almost 2 percent of the total US population. At the time of the 2020 census, only 0.88 percent of Americans lived in Kansas.[4] And when a state's population dwindles, so does its workforce, which detracts from businesses.

Kansas needed more people, and Wichita State needed more students. We needed Kansans to stay in Kansas, and perhaps even more specifically, more people had to come to Kansas to live and work, as Bardo said during a press conference: "Our interest is in making sure we keep the best and brightest people in Wichita so that they become part of our long-term workforce."[5]

To this end, the university hired a firm to assist with Strategic Enrollment Management (SEM) planning, positioning itself for long-term enrollment success. In Bardo fashion, he boiled it down in plain language: "The plan is to spend hundreds of thousands . . . the payoff will be millions."[6] It was a complete change in mindset, according to Dr. Shirley Lefever, who recalled:

> Prior to SEM, we just offered classes, and if the students came, awesome. We weren't intentional about our enrollment, and we certainly weren't strategic about it. Once SEM planning began, the deans were asked to establish enrollment goals, but initially we didn't know where to start that conversation. We began to have internal conversations about the relevance of degree programs, which then led to conversations with stakeholders about their needs.[7]

But once the conversations started, a whole new level of strategic thinking began about who we should recruit and how to support those students once they enroll, and no one was left out of the discussion.

The plan included eleven goals for Wichita State—ranging from creating a culture around student support and retention to recruiting out-of-state students and updating degree programming. Each goal was broken down into specific tactics with metrics as a guide to achievement.

At the time, I was working in the Office of Academic Affairs as an associate vice president. Bardo asked me to spearhead the development and implementation of the SEM plan. A SEM committee—of which I was a part—was formed to devise goals, strategies, and tactics. This was my sweet spot. I have a penchant for operationalizing the big picture and drilling into the details of how we get from idea to implementation.

"Strategic Enrollment Management at Wichita State University represents a profound cultural shift, building a stronger university and a more vibrant Kansas," said Dr. Ashlie Jack, associate vice president for institutional effectiveness and current leader of SEM. "Our strategic blueprint and driving vision unite faculty and staff in a university-wide initiative focused on enrollment growth, supporting all students with a consistent standard of care and academic advising, and bringing siloed offices together. It fosters a culture of sustainable and manageable growth that is student centered, turning big, bold goals into actionable steps."[8]

One of SEM's first priorities was to set the explicit expectation that this was a university-wide initiative. This was not a John Bardo plan, and it wasn't a Rick Muma plan. For Wichita State to achieve each of those eleven goals,[9] everyone—including every single member of our faculty, staff, and administration—had to be on board. We had to live and breathe all things SEM.

It was important to me that people understood this wasn't

a dog and pony show to demonstrate our bureaucratic savvy. This was a concerted effort to bring siloed offices together to strategically grow enrollment in ways that are manageable and sustainable.

We were relentless in driving home the SEM goals and tactics through town halls, internal and external newsletters, and faculty and staff meetings. I believed then, as I do today, that it's important to constantly stay on message. Repeat the goals, weave them into conversations, and create energy around a cause that we could collectively sink our teeth into—the advancement of Shocker Nation.

It worked. At the end of the five-year SEM plan in 2021, our enrollment had increased 7 percent,[10] which Dr. Carolyn Shaw, a professor of political science and a former SEM leader, described as quite a feat: "What we had accomplished is particularly impressive when compared with some other institutions, and we are very proud of our work and results."[11] One of the ways we grew so much was through the tactic of recruiting out-of-state students. To entice people to come to Kansas, we went way back to the pioneering days of covered wagons and cattle drives: the Chisholm Trail, which you might know today as the Interstate-35 corridor, connecting Wichita directly to major metropolises such as Oklahoma City, Dallas, Houston, Kansas City, and Des Moines. The strategy was outlined by Bardo in a 2016 op-ed piece in *The Wichita Eagle*:

Wichita and Kansas aren't growing at the pace of the Kansas City area or the metro areas to our south. If Wichita State can regularly draw students from all along the I-35 corridor, both the university and the regional economy will benefit. . . . The number of people here with college degrees must be increased. Because of the restructuring of the economy, it is crucial that our region be linked to larger hubs of trade and economic activity.[12]

Through the I-35 corridor strategy, Wichita State began offering in-state tuition to students from select cities in major metropolitan areas along the corridor, which we call Shocker Cities;[13] for students who live along the corridor, but outside those metropolitan areas, we offer a 33 percent tuition discount through our Shocker Select program.[14] We believed that students from Shocker Cities and Shocker Select areas would choose Wichita State and that a good chunk of them would choose to stay in Kansas. Bardo wrote at the time that 20 to 35 percent of out-of-state students at other universities stay in those cities upon graduation. As he stated, "Many others will return to their home metropolitan areas, but they take with them knowledge and relationships that can act as informal linkages in the development of regional networks."[15]

The idea was always to get students to Wichita State, get them connected to the community and to applied learning experiences, and eventually help them gain full-time employment with local industry after graduation.

By all measures, the I-35 strategy has been a tremendous success: Enrollment from Shocker Cities and Shocker Select states went from a little over four hundred students in 2010 to nearly fifteen hundred in 2024, an increase of 275 percent.[16]

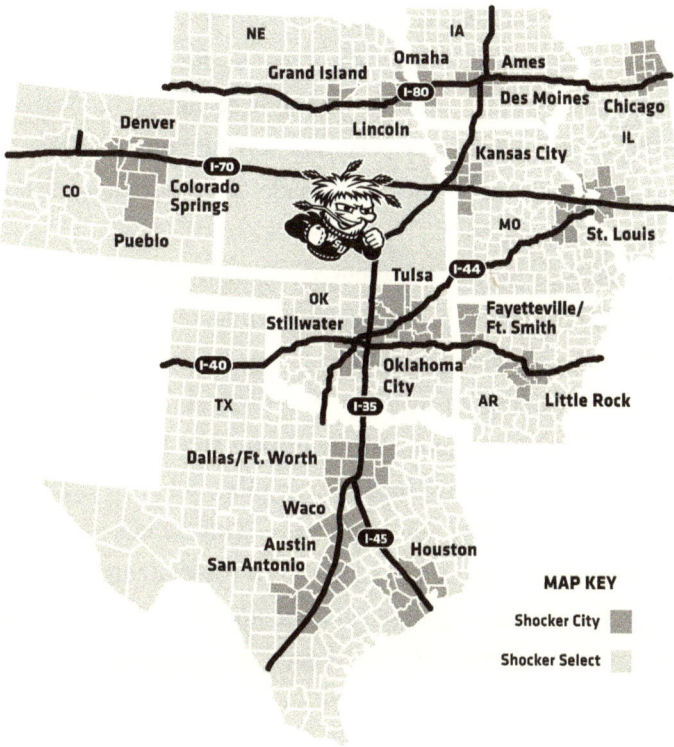

Recruiting out-of-state students via the I-35 Corridor Strategy.

And of the students from these areas who graduate from Wichita State, almost 50 percent stay in Kansas to live, work, and build connections to their communities.[17] That's compared with the 70 percent of all Wichita State undergraduate students who stay in Kansas after graduation—the highest rate for any university in the state, according to data from the Kansas Board of Regents.[18]

Our SEM strategies worked because we committed to the

plan. Even in our lean years and through years of state budget cuts and all the way to the present day, we funded the plan. In some cases, it was painful, as we had to reallocate funds from within. That meant some programs saw no budget increases, and in certain cases, cuts were made to areas that were not demonstrating growth.

Building an innovation-focused university is about building partnerships, research, new facilities and—most important—understanding who your students are and what they need to succeed. Being an urban public research university with a significant enrollment of low-income and first-generation students, it's imperative that we recognize, support, and fund the distinct needs of that population. This includes creating programs specifically targeted toward those students—including financial and need-based aid, mentoring, advising to help navigate the nuances of a university, academic support, and summer bridge programs.

We also created professional development for our faculty and staff, assisting them in changing the culture to one of enrollment, outreach, and advocacy, as well as providing more need-based aid from institutional sources, private resources, and the state. And we launched a very intense student success and persistence plan to support students with various wraparound services, once they were here, which included two new buildings: the Shocker Success Center (an all-inclusive facility with eighteen student support offices in the heart of campus) and the Shocker Career Accelerator (an annex added to the Marcus Welcome Center, for students to see and experience the full life cycle of what it means to be a Shocker the moment they show up on campus, from admission to career readiness).

We are now committed to investing 10 percent of tuition revenue toward SEM, and we've seen great success in both recruiting and retaining students.

But back to the growing pains and pushback. Frankly, this was hard work and often not very pretty. We did all of this in a relatively short period of time.

For example, we fully reorganized all enrollment offices from the Division of Student Affairs into the Division of Academic Affairs. This dramatic and sudden shift bred anxiety, and we lost some folks along the way—individuals who ultimately chose to pursue opportunities elsewhere. I hated that part of it, but I knew with this kind of change, it was inevitable.

I've always believed that enrollment happens at the college level and supported with student affairs' retention work. We knew if we could turn the ship toward growth, even ever so slightly, we would eventually bring new revenue sources to the institution to operate in an environment of growth—or at least not going backward. And so, we did.

## WHAT'S THE MAIN POINT?

To say that a university serves students is a no-brainer. To truly understand who those students are, where they're coming from, and how to best serve them—while also serving the community at large—is an exercise in adaptability. Moreover, it underscores the significance of strategic enrollment planning, which allows universities to proactively align resources, programs, and initiatives with the evolving needs of the student body and the broader community. Developing and implementing a thoughtful and actionable strategic enrollment plan allows leaders to effectively navigate the complexities of higher education and ensure that their efforts are both student centered and community focused, ultimately fostering success for all stakeholders.

## WHAT WE DID WELL

- The I-35 corridor strategy has been an unequivocal success, nearly quadrupling our enrollment from targeted out-of-state students since its implementation.
- We invested, and continue to invest, in the Strategic Enrollment Management plan and student success and persistence.
- Rather than brushing off the changing expectations of higher education, we adapted.

## LESSONS LEARNED

Our SEM plan gave us a new perspective on how to connect with prospective students, and it helped us focus programming and initiatives in a way we'd never done before. In large part, it's the reason we've been able to continue to grow.

**CONSIDERATIONS FOR THE READER**

- Do you have a strategic plan to grow enrollment? It's not as simple as saying, "We want more students." You'll find that creating an enrollment plan will help you understand who your students are, where they come from, and how to focus your energy and resources toward prospective populations that you might not have considered previously.
- Who is your student? Consider geographic origins, age range, family makeup, and financial status.
- How can you broaden your geographic outreach? Opportunities might include prospects from neighboring cities, states, or even bordering countries.
- Consider prospects who are outside of your typical recruitment outreach. Who is missing out on the opportunity to learn at your institution? This might include adult learners, international students, professionals looking to advance their careers, or people from varying socioeconomic groups.
- As you take inventory of your students and prospects, consider why some populations—from traditional eighteen-year-olds to lifelong learners—are missing out on the opportunity to learn at your institution. Are you age-friendly? Is there a financial barrier? Perhaps family responsibilities, a full-time job, or a long commute make in-person classes a struggle? Is it about the lack of applied learning experiences? How can you remove these barriers in a way that makes your institution accessible?

....................................................................................

**What to Expect in Chapter 7**

Wichita State University's applied learning model, which is seamlessly embedded in every degree program, adds dimension to our curriculum and makes our students more marketable when they graduate. In this chapter, I will explore our applied learning model and share insights into how this comprehensive approach to learning creates an agile and dynamic workforce for businesses in our region.

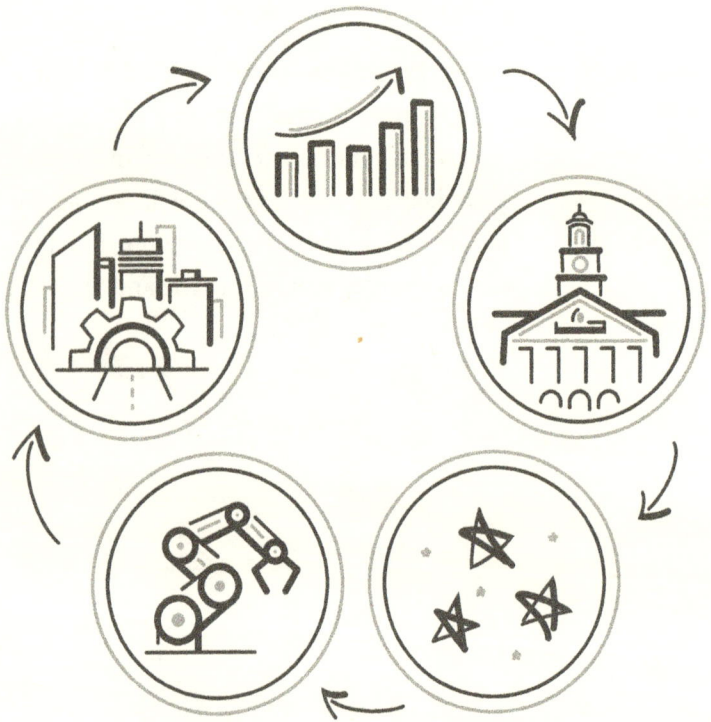

# 7

## Beyond Being an Employer, Driving Prosperity

We've created this talent ecosystem for our region that's for
the benefit of the student, the company, and the university.

I'm biased, of course, but I believe Wichita State is setting the
pace for the future of education. That's much of the impetus
behind writing this book and why I've dedicated the past three
decades of my life to growing this institution.

But if I were pressed to put my finger on an educational
method we do better than any other university, it would be our
applied learning model. When I ask parents why they're considering sending their child to WSU, they frequently mention
this learning model.

On the surface, applied learning, or learning by doing,
might not seem like anything special. Many institutions provide student internships and co-ops that help graduates learn
the ropes, build their résumés, and get a taste of their future
careers. But there *is* something special about applied learning
at WSU.

Prior to 2012, Wichita State—much like other higher education institutions—offered various internship programs that
encouraged students to pursue practical experiences. When
he became president, John Bardo took particular interest in

how internships were directed (quite successfully) by WSU's National Institute for Aviation Research (NIAR), where undergraduate students were fully integrated into research and development on major applied research projects. Students were immersed in meaningful work alongside career professionals, solving problems and assuming appropriate and increasing levels of responsibility.

When Wichita State created its strategic plan in 2013, it included the guarantee that all students would complete an applied learning experience as part of each degree program's curriculum. These applied learning experiences take many forms—including internships, project-based work, community service, and other opportunities that transcend the confines of traditional classrooms. Our objective was to better prepare industry-ready students by immersing them in real-world situations. The fact that we offer internships isn't novel; however, that every degree major we offer has a guaranteed applied learning or research experience baked right into it is cutting-edge. This safe and experimental development equips our students with relevant skills and experience, preparing them to be workforce-ready before graduation. It's our approach and commitment to applied learning that has been lauded by leaders of business and industry, students, alumni, and government officials. For example, in 2016, WSU partnered with a local advanced manufacturer that had planned to outsource a project overseas. The university developed and piloted a modified apprenticeship model in collaboration with the manufacturer, where undergraduate students digitized the plans for the manufacturer's priority project with accuracy and speed and at a cost that the manufacturer's outsourced engineers couldn't match.

Although this program was not created to offer permanent employment for the students, 35 percent ended up being extended job opportunities, and 83 percent found employment in the region after working on the project. The company estimated that Wichita State's approach to applied learning reduced time required for onboarding and training new engineers from two years to six months. This notable achievement stands as one of the key advantages often reported by companies that have collaborated with WSU's students. The significant reduction in onboarding and training times conserves valuable company resources and enables employers to swiftly respond to the evolving demands of the industry.

Clearly, this was a model that could be scaled for the benefit of all. Thus, it made sense to incorporate a modified apprenticeship into our model of applied learning, as Bardo wrote in "Innovation in the Heartland," an article published in 2019 in the journal *Issues in Science and Technology*: "Apprenticeships and longer-term internships can be important components of an overall strategy for STEM, but thinking differently about how to educate the students on campus also plays a critical role. That is why WSU's strategic plan calls for all students to have applied learning experiences, regardless of major."[1]

The benefits of our applied learning model are threefold: Students build their résumés and skill sets in a real-world environment (with most of them earning competitive wages);

companies benefit from work-ready students, dramatically reducing their onboarding expenditure for training newly graduated students; and our state benefits from this work-ready talent remaining in Kansas. The true strength of our model lies in how all the moving parts fit together to solve problems and create a system that fuels the education and innovation ecosystem.

When all of this was getting off the ground, I was working in the provost's office, and much of the implementation of this new initiative fell to my area. As a physician assistant, that's how I was educated. That immersive experience gave deeper meaning to what I learned from books and in the classroom, and it built my confidence and bridged my theoretical understanding with professional practice. So, it made sense to me that this applied learning model would also work for other fields of study.

Still, there were some faculty who remained skeptical. Some, such as Dr. George Dehner, a professor of history, felt that applied learning was something done at technical colleges and did not necessarily fall within the purview of what a university ought to do. As he stated, "We're not just the jobs place, we're a university, a higher education institution. We're not a technical school. We're not a community college. We need somebody who's teaching and helping our students to experience a much larger world than just skills. I'm not opposed to a talent pipeline of getting people trained and doing jobs, but that's not the be-all, end-all of the university."[2] While I understand Dr. Dehner's point of view, it's important to note that applied learning isn't focused solely on skill acquisition, as detailed in the WSU definition, according to our website, cocreated with and approved by the faculty:

> Applied learning at Wichita State is the application of learning to authentic situations. Applied learning occurs when students develop knowledge, skills, and values from personal direct experiences that go beyond the traditional lecture or lab. This synergistic relationship between classroom and applied learning experiences fosters critical thinking, reflective practices, and supports deep understanding of new knowledge, all while providing students with a heightened learning experience to support career readiness.

While applied learning opportunities may look different from one another, [they] share the following 3 components:

1. **Defined purpose:** Each applied learning engagement must have a defined approach and clear purpose. Beginning each engagement with intentionality and clear expectations between student and mentor/advisor maximizes the benefits, skills, and knowledge that will be gained for the student and establishes the solid foundation needed for success for all involved parties.
2. **Development of skills and competencies:** Each opportunity must focus on the participant developing skills, knowledge, and/or competencies that can be applied in authentic, professional/practical settings. Applied learning

engagements are frequently dynamic with changes made as the process unfolds. To facilitate continuous engagement, reflection and learning, the student engages in dialogue regarding outcomes, expectations, and opportunities to strengthen the experience.

3. **Assessment of outcomes and reporting:** The assessment of an applied learning experience should be focused on specific, measurable learning outcomes. Learning outcomes should be recorded in a manner that is easily understood and able to be reported. Students should also be provided with opportunities for reflection and self-assessment during the process to ensure they draw connections between the skills/knowledge from applied learning, their experience in the classroom, and situations they will encounter outside the classroom.[3]

Wichita State University's applied learning and research model is built on the fundamental belief that education should extend beyond traditional classroom lectures and laboratory experiments. Applied learning at Wichita State encompasses a diverse array of activities that equip students with knowledge, essential skills, and values through personal, direct experiences. These experiences extend far beyond the boundaries of traditional academia and provide students with a more holistic and practical understanding of their chosen fields of study.

Some examples include students who engage in work-based learning in Textron's Help Hangar, where they address IT issues for the company's employees;[4] or as engineering and technician students for the National Institute for Aviation Research; or as a team leader for Smart Factory by Deloitte @ Wichita. Still other instances involve engineering students who helped build a bridge in Ecuador;[5] physics students participating in research for NASA;[6] STEM students working at law firms doing patent research;[7] health professions students processing specimens in WSU's Molecular Diagnostics Laboratory;[8] anthropology students doing fieldwork for the City of Wichita;[9] or aerospace engineering students creating digital twins of military aircraft.[10] It's like reverse engineering the typical student experience, said Dr. Amy Drassen Ham, who explained:

> I want my students to be employed. I want them to get good jobs. I want them to graduate with successful skills—skills they were able to learn and practice in an applied way here at the university, where they can risk and try and seek and fail and get feedback in a safer environment—so that we're putting out graduates who are ready to contribute to the economy and ready to build our community.[11]

Bridging the gap between our educational philosophy and the tangible benefits it brings to our students, one particular point of pride for Wichita State is that the vast majority of our applied learning experiences are paid, said Bobby Gandu, associate vice president for strategic enrollment management and applied learning and director of admissions.[12] "Each year," according to Gandu, "Wichita State students earn over

$35 million across more than 9,000 paid applied learning positions including on-campus positions and research experiences, plus external internships with organizations and companies. Ultimately that means Shockers are not only gaining valuable professional experience that could catapult them to the front of the line for a post-college job offer; it also translates as income that students use toward maximizing college affordability."[13] Our students are earning a competitive wage through applied learning,[14] which contributes to tuition, books, and living expenses.

This is an important differentiator for Wichita State because we're an urban campus with a high ratio of students from low-income families who may not be able to pursue their academic goals without a well-paying job.[15] While unpaid internships might be the traditional and national norm, spending twenty hours a week in a job without getting paid is a privilege that few of our students can afford.

Traditionally, you might find college students working in restaurants or retail stores—all of which are solid employment options. However, getting a student's foot in the door of their area of academic interest helps them build the skills and knowledge necessary to make significant impacts in their future careers. And if they can do all this while earning an income, it helps students persist and achieve their academic and career goals.

Additionally, while students build their résumés, they're also gaining an intangible skill set: business acumen, leadership development, decision-making abilities, networking, communication skills, and professional connections. I call this professionalization. That's in addition to a stronger connection with their university, explained Dr. Teri Hall, vice president for student affairs. "One of the things I didn't expect from our applied learning emphasis was how internships and applied learning enhanced students' connection with WSU," she said. "Students' experiences and connections to their education expanded to the entire city and country. Applied learning helps with their pocketbook and employability and increases confidence and pride in their education."[16]

One avenue for students to find applied learning opportunities is through WSU's Shocker Career Accelerator (SCA). The SCA helps connect students with professional opportunities by assisting employers in posting job openings, targeting students for right-fit roles, and facilitating networking through career fairs and workshops. While the SCA supports students in building résumés, practicing interviews, and creating effective LinkedIn profiles, the responsibility for hiring, onboarding, and training falls primarily on the SCA once students apply for these positions.

Programs such as Tutor 316 provide a strong example of how the university manages employment logistics and payroll for applied learning. Tutor 316 is an SCA initiative through which students are hired as WSU employees to serve as tutors in local schools, addressing a community need while gaining valuable applied learning experience. This program represents a targeted way SCA supports both students and community partnerships, according to Hall, who explained, "These students not only build skills but also give back to the community, embodying the spirit of applied learning at WSU."[17]

In broader contexts, WSU's Ennovar (a derivative of the Spanish word *innovar*, which means to innovate) program specializes in applied learning placements that involve university-facilitated hiring and training. Ennovar serves as a talent ecosystem, connecting students with industry opportunities while managing hiring logistics, insurance, and payroll. If a placement isn't a good fit, Ennovar works to replace the student, retrain as necessary, and ensure the partnership remains strong.

All these advantages combine to create a robust talent pipeline of highly employable Shocker graduates who can make an immediate and meaningful contribution to Kansas businesses and industries, explained Tonya Witherspoon, WSU's former associate vice president for industry engagement: "We've created this talent ecosystem that's for the benefit of the student, the region, and the university."[18]

Let me provide an example of our applied learning model in action. In 2021, Wichita State's NIAR program partnered with a private aircraft modification firm to conduct the research and convert a Boeing 777 passenger plane into a cargo plane. This was done under the umbrella of NIAR's Maintenance, Repair and Overhaul (MRO) program. The NIAR MRO program employs WSU and WSU Tech students for applied learning— including those studying engineering, finance, management, and business—and employs many full-time, salary-earning, taxpaying, benefits-eligible workers.

The program has been overwhelmingly successful as we partner with companies to convert aircraft, such as the A321, Boeing 737, and MD-80, for cargo and special-missions modifications.

If you're keeping score: That's a win for hundreds of students each year who are earning income, expanding their educational journey, and building their résumés, a win for our business partners, who benefit from WSU's aviation and engineering expertise, and a win for the Kansas economy, which gets a boost from the private and government investment and employment opportunities.

I could go on and on about the benefits of our applied learning model, but I'll end this chapter with the words of some of our students, business partners, and national leaders:

- Keegan Staats, an economics student who worked at the National Institute for Aviation Research during his junior year at Wichita State: "I do not know about many other job opportunities a college student would have that can give them the exact kind of experience they would be expected to need at a normal job. NIAR seems to treat its student-workers as real employees by actively teaching and growing their abilities to perform tasks related to their major and desired career path."[19]
- The Honorable Sethuraman Panchanathan, former director of the National Science Foundation: "Wichita State University is doing amazing things. When I look at the convergence of what industry needs and what we need to train

the next generation of experts, that fusion is right here in action—live—which is phenomenal to watch."[20]

- Alia Michaelis, a biochemistry student who worked as an emergency medical scribe for the Wichita location of Ascension Medical Group, one of the nation's leading non-profit and Catholic health systems, during her junior year: "The amount of on-the-job learning that I am doing is incredible, as I can learn from the doctors with whom I work and who love to teach everything and anything about medicine. For medical school applications, clinical experience is a requirement, and I definitely feel as though I am getting great clinical experience in my current position."[21]

- Jason Bergstrom, Smart Manufacturing senior commercial adviser leader and principal for Deloitte Consulting LLP: "We are incredibly fortunate to have access to the student talent at Wichita State. While we're here at the Smart Factory @ Wichita by Deloitte to help them learn more about smart manufacturing and business, they also are significant resources to us as they are currently learning the newest approaches to technological deployments, business strategy, and more. Their perspectives continue to help us understand how the next generation of manufacturing leaders will approach solving challenges in the industry."[22]

## WHAT'S THE MAIN POINT?

Certainly, the education students receive in the classroom is foundational, but it's often the real-world applications and hands-on experiences that bridge the gap between theory and practice. Practical exposure—such as internships, research projects, co-op programs, and our very own version of applied learning experiences—can provide invaluable insights into their future careers. These experiences allow students to see how their classroom knowledge is put into action and help them gain a deeper understanding of the challenges and opportunities that await them after graduation. In essence, applied learning is the missing puzzle piece that empowers students to envision and prepare for their future professional journey.

## WHAT WE DID WELL

- Wichita State formalized the requirement that all degree majors include applied learning.
- With an emphasis on paid applied learning, many of our students can pay for their education and living expenses while working and continuing their education. We convinced the Kansas legislature to invest so that we could offer more paid experiences.
- Business and industry leaders often comment that Wichita State students are their go-to resource when hiring new employees because of their professionalism and preparedness.
- Our distinctive applied learning model gives us a competitive edge in attracting students who are eager to gain real-world experience while they earn their degrees.

## LESSONS LEARNED

Gone are the days when our universities were siloed institutions for the pursuit of education solely for the sake of knowledge. We'd be remiss as university leaders if we didn't help our students prepare for their future careers in every manner possible, and that includes giving them a realistic understanding of the work environment. When we insist on applied learning experiences for all, we allow our students to explore the practical applications of the professional skills they're building in the classroom.

## CONSIDERATIONS FOR THE READER

- I'm sure you currently have students who work at internships and co-ops. How can you expand those experiences to include more students—perhaps even all your students?
- Are there partnerships you have that you might leverage to create more experiential opportunities for your students?
- Consider the organizations on campus and in your community. What challenges do they have? Can your students work to solve those problems through research or internship opportunities?
- Are there immersive opportunities your students can experience to give them a more wholistic understanding of their future careers?

........................................................................................

**What to Expect in Chapter 8**

At Wichita State University, our role as a public institution is a pledge to the people of our state, and we are wholly dedicated to advancing and improving the well-being of our community. For us, that means listening to our students and creating avenues of access that meet their educational goals. Our affiliation with a local technical college has expanded the options for students, allowing them to get the individual educational experience that fits their life circumstances. As you read this chapter, consider how partnerships can help you enhance community engagement, diversify student populations, and forge effective partnerships for educational and community development.

# 8

## What's In It for Everyone?

Everyone can find a place within Shocker Nation.
With a pathway from GED to PhD.

Many universities boast about their rigid admittance criteria and low acceptance rates, emphasizing their selectiveness and exclusivity. It works for them. But our steadfast dedication to our community demands that we take a different approach at Wichita State: We prioritize accessibility and are committed to the people we serve. As an urban public research university, we must be accountable; it's our privilege—and, quite deliberately, our moral mandate—to create opportunities that enhance the lives of the people and communities we serve.

For us, it's not only about increasing enrollment—though that is, to be sure, an important metric for understanding how well we are serving our students. What really drives us at Wichita State is creating pathways for our students to achieve their dreams.

Far too often, a person's dreams are dashed because higher education seems out of reach. Maybe it seems like something *other* people do—other people who have better grades, more money, better circumstances, or stronger family support. As educational leaders, we have an opportunity to show them their potential, to kindle their hopes and ambitions, and introduce them to possibilities.

But not everyone wants, needs, or is prepared for a university education. There's more than one way to build a career, and the pursuit of a bachelor's or graduate degree isn't the only route to success. It was with this in mind that Wichita State decided to expand its reach and leverage its innovative spirit to create a pathway for students to achieve success—however they might define it—on their own terms.

In 2015, WSU began working with administrators from Wichita Area Technical College (WATC) to formalize a partnership to increase the availability and quality of opportunities for students while directly meeting the core workforce needs of the state.[1] It made sense. Both institutions already had a solid foundation of applied learning with a commitment to solving problems for the community. We already had transfer agreements in place for students from WATC to transfer to Wichita State, and we were frequent project collaborators.

The first proposal was to completely merge the two institutions,[2] but as Dr. Sheree Utash, then president of WATC, explained that there was internal and external resistance along the way: "Dr. Bardo and I went to Topeka [the capital city of Kansas], and we thought that we had a slam dunk. Out of left field, some of the community colleges blasted the idea of a merger. They were totally against it. Several community colleges voiced concerns that if Wichita State began offering two-year degrees and certificates, it would impact their market share and bottom line."[3] Their worry was that students might choose the expanded offerings of Wichita State rather than opt for community college. After some debate, those concerns were enough to stall momentum at the state level. Senate Bill 451 ultimately died in committee. But Wichita State and WATC were undeterred. Rather than backing down, we saw the setback as an opportunity to reevaluate, refocus, and find a new path forward. The goal wasn't competition. It was collaboration in service of students and the regional workforce. By continuing to pursue creative solutions, we remained committed to a vision that would ultimately lead to greater access, stronger partnerships, and a more responsive higher education ecosystem for Kansas.

After realizing their initial plan wouldn't move forward as expected, the two leaders found themselves regrouping in Topeka. As Utash recalled, "I remember that Dr. Bardo and I were walking out the door and getting on the elevator and both of us looking at each other, and we said, 'Well, we'll just figure out how to do it.' That's how we went from merger to affiliation, which was really a blessing in my mind. I think it was the right thing to do."[4]

In July 2018, after thirty months and a great deal of work, the Higher Learning Commission (the accrediting body for Wichita State) approved the affiliation, and WATC's name and governance officially changed. Wichita Area Technical College became the Wichita State University Campus of Applied Sciences and Technology,[5] also known as WSU Tech.[6] Governance was switched from the Sedgwick County Technical Education and Training Authority to the Kansas Board of Regents, which also governs WSU. Utash became president of WSU Tech and vice president of workforce development for WSU, a position that reports to the Wichita State president. In essence, we created a Wichita State system, with its main campus and the new WSU Tech campus. This affiliation established a nimble relationship within the Wichita State system and unlocked opportunities for students seeking to further their knowledge, skill set, trade, or professional development.

Through the affiliation, everyone can find a place within Shocker Nation. With a pathway from GED to PhD, Wichita State can meet students where they are, learn their career goals, and create a plan for achievement. At WSU Tech, students can obtain an associate of applied science degree and technical certificates in fields as diverse as culinary arts, aviation maintenance, professional piloting, architect design technology, criminal justice, nursing, and surgical technology.[7]

Meanwhile, students can seamlessly apply their general education credits toward a Wichita State degree, giving them the opportunity to pursue a bachelor's degree or even advance to graduate studies. It's not uncommon for Wichita State students to also take classes at WSU Tech after earning their bachelor's degree—either immediately after finishing their degree or after years on the job market—to retool, retrain, or earn specialized certifications. Dr. John Tomblin, executive vice president for Research and Industry and Defense Programs, and WSU's NIAR executive director, said, "Anyone who wants to advance themselves can come to Wichita State and WSU Tech to learn a skill, earn a degree, and build a career. It's an opportunity that is available to anyone and everyone, no matter where you are in your education or career path."[8] WSU Tech conducts extensive work with area high schools, offering workforce training for college credit. It's an open-access institution with no qualified admissions.[9] This means that even if someone drops out of high school, WSU Tech has programming to help them prepare to take the GED exam, which will allow them to pursue educational opportunities and careers previously unavailable to them. As Utash explained, "So, all of a sudden, there was a place for everyone to get an education. There were doors open for everyone from every level of academic success they may or may not have had, to be able to build a career based on education, and that was not there before."[10] In a 2017 *Wichita Business Journal* podcast, *BizTalk with Bill Roy*, Utash said: "This affiliation allows us to be greater together than apart, and it's going to allow us to build for this community an opportunity for applied sciences and degrees at the bachelor's degree level through WSU."[11] Building on Utash's vision for the community, WSU President Bardo emphasized in a news release at the time that "the economic success of this state is at the very heart of what Wichita State does and informs every decision that we make. This is a natural partnership that ensures the state of Kansas remains competitive with its neighbors and attractive to companies looking to explore new approaches to innovation, creativity, and research."[12]

Since the affiliation launched in 2018, the relationship between the two institutions has evolved and deepened in ways that serve our students, the business community, and the overall prosperity of our region. Beyond transfer credits and coursework, WSU and WSU Tech partner on a myriad of projects to provide students with applied learning opportunities and to solve problems for people and industries.

Collaborative projects between the two entities are expansive and diverse; they include the Maintenance Repair and Overhaul program mentioned in chapter 5 and an initiative to address the teacher shortage by offering scholarships to WSU Tech students interested in educational careers.[13] In addition, Wichita State, WSU Tech, and the University of Kansas are building the Wichita Biomedical Campus, an academic health science center in downtown Wichita, to revolutionize health care education in Kansas and meet the demand for additional medical professionals in our region—from entry-level health care workers all the way to postgraduate medical education, something that is unique among health science centers.[14] Like the Innovation Campus, the biomedical campus's vision is to create another economic ecosystem, but one that is focused on health.

Zach Gearhart, chief of staff and executive director of government relations, explained that one particular strength of WSU Tech is its rapid responsiveness to the needs of business and industry: "WSU Tech is really innovative in creating new programs that are developed alongside industry."[15] While the affiliation makes sense for our students and our community, it also makes good business sense for the future of both institutions.

Universities in the United States are on the precipice of

Wichita State University and the University of Kansas have partnered to build the Wichita Biomedical Campus in downtown Wichita. This rendering shows Phase I of the campus, which is expected to open in 2027.

dealing with the total US birthrate falling by about 16 percent since between 2007 and 2024, according to the Centers for Disease Control.[16] Doing the math, that means between 2025 and 2028, there will be a steep decline in the pool of seventeen- and eighteen-year-olds to enroll at our nation's universities.

As we approach that cliff, one objective of the Wichita State and WSU Tech affiliation is to mitigate the impact of that impending enrollment challenge. Statistics show that roughly 45 percent of high school grads will immediately enroll in a four-year institution,[17] and about 17 percent will enroll in community college or technical school.[18] Rather than reaching only 45 percent of graduating high school seniors, WSU Tech's offerings allow us to cast a wider net; now, Wichita State can offer an array of educational opportunities to a diverse population of students who have varying educational needs.

Recognizing the urgency of this demographic shift, the Wichita community—including faculty, students, and local stakeholders—rallied around the affiliation as a proactive solution. Support for the partnership was broad and enthusiastic, reflecting a shared commitment to expanding educational access and opportunity. To build an inclusive opportunity-based educational ecosystem, the community seemed largely in favor of the partnership, including our Wichita State faculty, who voted heavily in favor of the affiliation.[19]

Community comments on social media included the following: "Quality education doesn't have to mean a traditional four-year degree. WATC and WSU have come together to give opportunities for a variety of students";[20] and "I think this is a fantastic opportunity for students following a skilled-trades path to be able to integrate into the WSU campus and expand their knowledge beyond their chosen trade . . . and include some basic accounting, marketing, business management, IT, and human resources knowledge to become better prepared to one day be a business owner or manager."[21]

## WHAT'S THE MAIN POINT?

The affiliation between Wichita State University and WSU Tech represents a compelling shift in higher education philosophy, one that prioritizes accessibility and community impact over exclusivity and traditional pathways. By merging innovation with a commitment to serve the needs of both students and industries, this partnership creates a dynamic educational enterprise where individuals from all backgrounds can find their place and pursue their aspirations. Through seamless integration of technical training and academic advancement, Wichita State can now offer a comprehensive range of opportunities, from technical certificates to doctoral degrees, ensuring that every student has the support and resources to achieve success on their own terms. This collaborative approach addresses the evolving demands of our workforce and strengthens the economic vitality of our region, positioning Wichita State as a leader in forging a brighter future for all.

## WHAT WE DID WELL

- We recognized the value of technical education and the importance of transitions between WSU Tech and Wichita State, ensuring students have flexible educational pathways.
- The affiliation model has enabled students to take a learn-as-you-grow approach, allowing them to upskill and adapt throughout their careers.
- Our partnership strengthened the workforce by equipping students with both technical expertise and higher education credentials, benefiting industries and businesses.

- We listened to our students and community, adapting to their needs by developing an innovative educational ecosystem that serves learners from GED to PhD.

## LESSONS LEARNED

When we affiliated with WATC, we increased our reach, and we're promoting access to higher education to a wider breadth of prospects. The affiliation wasn't easy or without bumps along the way. In the end, though, it has increased our footprint in the community and provided students with on- and off-ramps for education, certification, and professional development.

## CONSIDERATIONS FOR THE READER

- Do the admittance policies at your university align with your mission and vision? For instance: Does your mission statement put emphasis on accessibility and affordability, while stringent acceptance policies put barriers on who is admitted?
- How can you create access opportunities for your students while simultaneously creating opportunities for your university and industry partners?
- Are there educational institutions in proximity to your school that would help you build a broader menu of educational experiences?

........................................................................................

## What to Expect in Chapter 9

Clear and consistent communication about priorities is essential to activating an institution's vision and ensuring that everyone is on the same page. However, it's not enough to simply have priorities. Those priorities need to be shared clearly, consistently, and often. In this chapter, you'll learn about Wichita State's strategic priorities, how we arrived at them, and how we communicate them. At Wichita State, our priorities are ubiquitous. They are a central role in every speech I deliver and every initiative we build. They are the building blocks for the future of the university. As you think about your institution's priorities, consider how they serve your constituents and how you communicate them to a wider audience. As you delve into this chapter, it's my hope—and the intent of this book—that our story will inspire you to shape a brighter future for your institution and stakeholders.

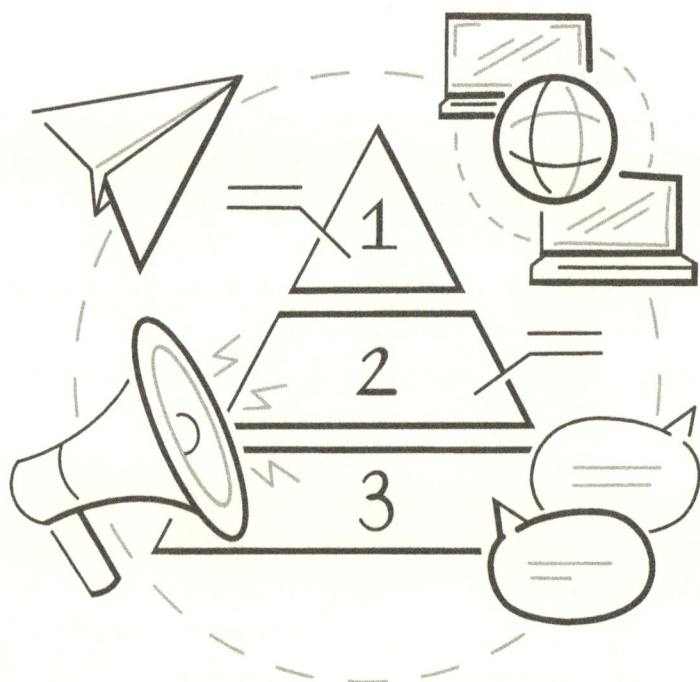

# 9

## Everything Comes Down to Priorities

Leaders must always provide clear communication
without nuances, addenda, or capitulations.

University leaders are akin to conductors, orchestrating a symphony of elements: students, faculty, staff, alums, meetings, speaking engagements, research, governing boards, events, and the multitude of other dynamic components demanding our unwavering focus and synchronization to safeguard the university's prosperity and ongoing expansion.

It would be easy to get lost in the cacophony of it all. Without clear communication, we would be navigating through chaos. Leaders must always provide clear communication without nuances, addenda, or capitulations.

Reflecting on Wichita State University's transformative journey, a foundational theme emerges: Clear and consistent communication around our strategic plan has united our diverse stakeholders and provided a shared sense of direction. It clarifies where we've been, where we are, and where we aspire to go. While the strategic plan sets the long-range vision, I have embraced three core priorities, as quoted from our university website, that translate our vision into a practical and memorable road map:

- Helping families through access and affordability.
- Supporting businesses with a talent pipeline that meets employer needs.
- Increasing economic prosperity with higher education to benefit the economy.[1]

Readers may have noted those ideas peppered throughout this book's chapters. These priorities are communicated with simplicity and consistency and become the touchstones aligning our community. I saturate my communications with them and build the future of the university around them. They're mantras that help me focus on what's important and guide my leadership journey, especially when faced with challenges like a pandemic or changes brought about by government. Access and affordability, talent pipeline, economic prosperity . . .

And it's not just me. You'd be hard-pressed to find a member of our faculty or staff who can't repeat these priorities—whether they agree with them or not. The simplicity of the message resonates across all levels of leadership and throughout every department and division across campus, fostering a unified front.

Let me step back for a moment and mention John Bardo again. There's no question that he was a great visionary. He saw the potential in Wichita State, and he made things happen; we would not be where we are today without his determination and vision. To carry forward and accelerate where Dr. Bardo left off, I focused on clear and simple communication, which I know is important in a strong leader. My communication abilities can be attributed to my training and clinical work as a physician assistant. Like my approach as a health care professional, where clear communication was paramount in conveying treatment plans to patients or population-based approaches to health care as a public health practitioner, my role as a university president requires a comparable level of steady and thoughtful communication. In health care, it was about effectively communicating priorities for patients or the health of communities. Now, as a university president, it's about articulating and organizing priorities that drive the success of Wichita State. The ability to distill complex information, provide clarity, and rally support is a skill set I transferred from my health care background to the realm of higher education leadership.

Emphasizing the three priorities is most pronounced during celebrations of success and milestones. By showcasing achievements that align with access, talent pipeline growth, and regional economic impact, I reinforced the shared commitment and invigorated the collective spirit for future endeavors. And when we suffer setbacks or challenges, we learn from the missteps, adapt our strategies, and use our priorities to get us back on track and propel us forward.

It's my belief that my consistent and clear messaging instills confidence, sets parameters and expectations, and creates alignment among staff and faculty members at Wichita State.

Wichita State's priorities were developed as part of our own strategic planning process and align closely with the Kansas Board of Regents' strategic plan,[2] which provides guidance for the state's thirty-two public universities, community colleges, and technical colleges. The priorities work in concert to help our students and our state thrive and succeed.

## ACCESS AND AFFORDABILITY

There's no more succinct mandate of what an urban public research university ought to do than create affordable and accessible higher education for the people we serve, and much of our success hinges on this priority.

Our excellence is based on the opportunities we create for the people we serve. We pride ourselves on helping people break down barriers, supporting their goals and helping them achieve success—however they might define it.

It's not all about enrolling students at Wichita State University. Our growing enrollment indicates that our focus on helping students persist in their academic careers, grow as people, overcome their struggles, and realize their potential is the right thing to do. There's no one-size-fits-all approach to persistence and retention in higher education, and in the past few years, Wichita State has amped up its efforts to boost student achievement with support resources.[3]

What we know is that one of the most significant reasons students drop out of college—or choose not to pursue higher education—is money.[4] The overwhelming cost of higher education can feel insurmountable to many families. To add to that, Kansas ranks as one of the least-funded states for our

**Need-based aid for workforce and talent**

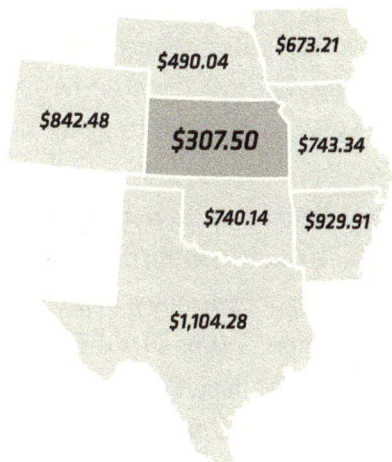

$490.04

$673.21

$842.48

$307.50

$743.34

$740.14

$929.91

$1,104.28

Need-based aid for work-force and talent, per full-time equivalency spending on need-based aid. Source: compiled by Kansas Board of Regents, 2025.

students' need-based aid.[5] With this in mind, when I became president, I made need-based aid my top focus.

By increasing support in this area, we aim to alleviate the financial burdens our students may encounter, ensuring that finances are not a barrier to their educational aspirations.

As we strive to alleviate these financial burdens, we remain steadfast in our commitment to meeting students where they are and supporting their individual journeys. We focus on understanding their barriers and helping them achieve their academic and career goals. I encourage our faculty and staff to assume good faith when a student is struggling and to act with empathy. We should not assume that a failing student is un-motivated or inattentive, when it might be that the student is working two jobs to support their family and is just exhausted.

Student persistence is about our responsibility to our

students and our community. It's about being good stewards of the trust that our students put in us when they enroll at Wichita State. They trust us to help them achieve their academic goals and realize their potential.

We have a moral imperative to do the right thing for our students.

At Wichita State, success is defined in more than 23,000 ways.[6] For some students, success means getting the very best grades, joining clubs, seizing every opportunity that comes their way, and getting the job of their dreams after they graduate. For others, it might mean taking the brave step of being the first in their family to attend college or making a deadline on an assignment while juggling family responsibilities and a full-time job.

Each of our students braves success on their own set of challenges and barriers—whether they be academic, financial, or related to prioritizing their mental and physical health. Our job as a university is to help them find the program that fits their needs and steward them through the resources available to help them succeed.

## FUELING THE TALENT PIPELINE

Our first priority of access and affordability might seem like an obvious goal for a public university, but some might question why we would put so much focus on building a talent pipeline for employers. The answer is twofold: First, we obviously want our students to find careers upon graduation; second, as mentioned earlier, as a public institution, we are accountable to the community and state we serve, and that translates to preparing today's students for the industry of tomorrow in our region. Of course, not everyone agrees, such as Dr. George Dehner, Wichita State professor of history, who stated, "I think the idea that we're here to get students jobs—that's not the primary goal of higher education."[7] This perspective, expressed by Dr. Dehner, reflects a concern shared by some faculty who view the role of higher education as broader than workforce preparation. However, it is undeniable that the majority of students pursue higher education to secure gainful employment.[8] Gone are the days when the primary motivation for pursuing a college education was intellectual curiosity. The contemporary landscape of academia demands that the substantial investment made in one's higher education should invariably translate into a tangible and rewarding return on investment.

As we prepare students to be the leaders of tomorrow, we are building a robust talent pipeline alongside employers in our region. Through our rigorous curriculum, student support programs, and an applied learning model, we help ensure Shocker graduates are ready to make meaningful and immediate contributions once they graduate.

Our educational ecosystem benefits our students, and it ensures that Kansas remains competitive in the global economy. By equipping our graduates with the skills and practical experience needed to excel in their chosen fields, we fulfill their aspirations and strengthen the talent of our region. Ultimately, our commitment to both access and affordability, as well as preparing students for successful careers, aligns with the broader goals of progress and economic prosperity. In following this approach, we continue to uphold our duty to serve the community and contribute to the growth and development of the state of Kansas.

## ECONOMIC PROSPERITY

Our final priority, economic prosperity, is really the culmination of the first two: When we give people access to postsecondary education and they use that education to benefit their overall quality of life through well-paying careers at companies needing a skilled and educated workforce to grow, the entire state benefits.

Again, though a state's economic prosperity might not be what some people consider falling under the purview of what a university traditionally does, I truly believe that it's what a public university ought to do. We are so intricately linked to our state and community, that their success is our success.

As creators and drivers of innovation, technology, and research, universities are in a unique position to be problem solvers and invest those capabilities into addressing some of the most pressing challenges facing society. And we'd be remiss if we didn't.

Our mission to boost economic prosperity is about fostering an interconnected ecosystem where our students, our

**104%**
increase in
four years

$392M

$366M

$261M

$192M

2021            2022            2023            2024

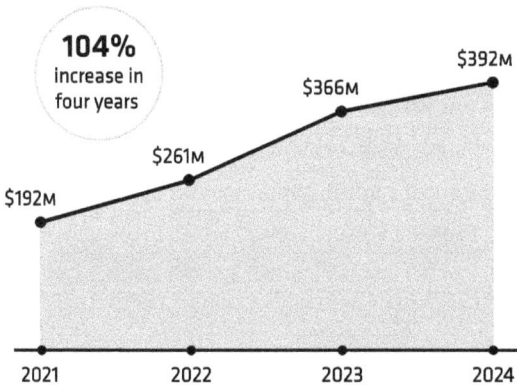

Wichita State University annual research expenditures
from 2021 to 2024.

institutions, and our state all thrive. By equipping our students
with the knowledge and skills they need for high-demand careers, we empower them to contribute to Kansas's economic
growth and stability. Moreover, as universities, we possess the
tools and expertise to tackle complex problems, drive innovation, and push the boundaries of knowledge. We have a responsibility to invest our capabilities in addressing the pressing
challenges of our time, for the betterment of our communities
and society at large. In doing so, we fulfill our role as catalysts
of progress and prosperity, shaping a brighter future for all.

## WHAT'S THE MAIN POINT?

As much as we'd like to, we can't be everything to everyone.
For any institution to do the most amount of good, it must

narrow its focus to meet its stakeholders' needs. Wichita State's priorities are expressed through very clear, consistent, and focused communication. In embracing our priorities, Wichita State University goes beyond academia. We're architects of access, champions of a talent pipeline, and catalysts for economic prosperity.

## WHAT WE DID WELL

- The university community has embraced the priorities of accessible and affordable education for families, building the talent pipeline for businesses and increasing Kansas's economic prosperity.
- We use clear and consistent language to our internal and external stakeholders, so everyone understands and is working toward our priorities.
- We built our priorities around our standing as Kansas's only urban public research university.
- We aligned our focus with three succinct priorities, effectively addressing and advancing our mission, our strategic plan, and the Kansas Board of Regents' strategic plan.

## LESSONS LEARNED

- Just because you say something doesn't mean it sticks. Say what you mean often and in bite-size chunks.

- Make talking points simple and consistent. Don't alter or cloud the message; it's confusing to people when you do. People like to know what the parameters are, even if they don't agree with them.

## CONSIDERATIONS FOR THE READER

- What are your priorities? How do they advance the vision and mission of your institution?
- How do you communicate your priorities with your constituencies: students, faculty, staff, alumni, the community, and the world?
- Does your university community embrace its priorities by weaving them into the day-to-day work of the institution? For instance: Are staff and faculty building curriculum, initiatives, and programs that advance your priorities?

# Conclusion

· · · · · · · · · · · · · · · · · · · · · · · · · · · · · · · · · · · · · · · · · · · · · · · · · · · · · · · · · ·

Here we are, in 2025, roughly a decade since the Innovation Campus was first envisioned. What began as an ambitious idea has transformed the very fabric of Wichita State, allowing us to achieve more than we could have ever imagined. It's changed the course of our university's future. Alumni often share their amazement when they return to a campus that has evolved beyond recognition—what was once a quiet, midsize research university is now a hub of innovation and progress.

We've prioritized affordability and access and continued year-over-year enrollment growth by investing millions in student need-based aid, launched a student success and persistence initiative, and transformed the physical aspect of the campus with the Innovation Campus, and we are now building a new biomedical campus. In just the past two years, we've opened Woolsey Hall, home of the W. Frank Barton School of Business; opened the Shocker Success Center, an all-inclusive student support center located in the heart of campus; opened the Marcus Welcome Center's Milly Marcus Annex, which showcases and provides services for the full Shocker experience from admission to career; and grew research expenditures

The Shocker Success Center at Wichita State University is a vibrant hub dedicated to student support and achievement, providing resources and services designed to help every Shocker thrive.

by 104 percent to a total of $392 million from 2021 to 2024. Our applied learning model has grown exponentially, with over nine thousand students collectively earning more than $35 million in just one year. Much more has happened along the way, and none of it would have been possible without a change in mindset.

Do you remember where, at the beginning of the book, I shared that long before I became president of Wichita State, I was just a young kid, running through campus while visiting my grandparents who worked here? Well, two things about that: First, almost every morning, one of my first thoughts is how I went from that wide-eyed kid exploring the campus to

Inside the Marcus Welcome Center at Wichita State, this dynamic hallway leads to the Milly Marcus Annex and the Shocker Career Accelerator—spaces dedicated to innovation, applied learning, and empowering students for career success.

now leading it as president. Second, I still run around these grounds—though I do more walking than running these days—seeing the incredible transformation of our students and the campus itself. I'm often in awe of what we've built together, and sometimes I can't believe it's real. And if you ask my spouse, Wichita State's first First Gentleman Rick Case, he'll tell you—I'm always dragging him along, as often as I can, just to soak it all in.

Hopefully, by now, you've surmised that I have a deep affinity for all things Wichita State. I am so proud of the relentless dedication and commitment of everyone in Shocker Nation. As I also wrote earlier, I was born to be a Shocker, and

Wichita State President Rick Muma and First Gentleman Rick Case visit a herd of goats that helped clear the land for the future Hub for Advanced Manufacturing Research building on the Innovation Campus.

I'm immensely honored and humbled to be at the helm of this great institution.

Over the past three decades, I've had the honor of watching our institution grow from a more traditional model to one that fiercely embraces innovation at every opportunity—in the classroom, through strategic partnerships, for our community and state, and with advanced problem-solving research. We are a university with clear priorities and a road map for excellence, as well as a will to persevere through the challenges and obstacles that might lie ahead.

In facing upcoming challenges, we're not just weathering

**Fall semester headcount of Wichita State University and its forerunners from 1895, and WSU Tech from 2003**

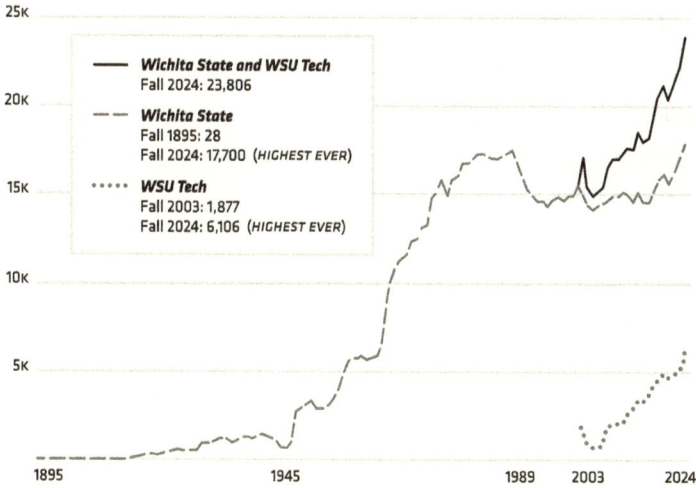

Wichita State University enrollment growth from 1895 to 2024.

the storm but actively charting a course for continued success. Our commitment to our students, innovation, and academic excellence remains unwavering. So, while we acknowledge the significance of these historic milestones, our eyes are firmly set on the future, ready to navigate the changing landscape with resilience and purpose.

Our mindset: We are student-centered and innovation-driven.

I hope you've enjoyed hearing my perspective on Wichita State's transformation. My wish is that elements of my reflection and the lessons I've shared inspire you to advance your goals and, in turn, contribute to the vital mission of public higher education—expanding access for all and driving our nation's economic prosperity.

Here's to the next chapter in our journey of excellence together. And to our Shocker community, thank you for being part of the momentum.

Go Shockers!

# Acknowledgments

· · · · · · · · · · · · · · · · · · · · · · · · · · · · · · · · · · · · · · · · · · · · · · · · ·

Writing a book is always a joint effort, and I am deeply grateful to everyone who helped turn this idea into reality.

I would like to thank the Wichita State University Strategic Communications and Marketing team for its countless hours of work ensuring this book meets the highest standards of quality. Thank you for your ideas, patience, and belief in the importance of telling this story.

To the numerous current and past faculty and staff at Wichita State University who were so giving of their time during interviews and reflections on the past ten-plus years at WSU.

Thank you to my colleagues, past and present, including those on the executive team, who were kind enough to read the many iterations of this book and provide your honest feedback. Your thoughts undoubtedly have resulted in a stronger, more meaningful book that captures the true story of our university and its impact. Without you, the university would not be what it is today.

To my readers—thank you for your curiosity in reading about the Wichita State University journey and for considering how it may inspire positive change in higher education.

To my grandparents Mary and Edward Blowers, who worked at WSU and let me tag along to campus in the summers, sealing my love of this great university.

And, finally, to every student who has walked the halls of this university. Your passion for learning, perseverance, and dreams for a brighter tomorrow continue to shape its future.

# Notes

**PREFACE**

1. Jon Marcus, "A Looming 'Demographic Cliff': Fewer College Students and Ultimately Fewer Graduates," NPR, Jan. 25, 2025, https://www.npr.org/2025/01/08/nx-s1-5246200/demographic-cliff-fewer-college-students-mean-fewer-graduates.

2. "Wichita State, WSU Tech Celebrate Highest Historical Enrollments," Wichita State University, Sept. 27, 2023, https://www.wichita.edu/about/wsunews/news/2023/09-sept/enrollment_1.php; "Board of Regents Announces 2023 Fall Semester Enrollment," news release, Kansas Board of Regents, Sept. 27, 2023, https://www.kansasregents.org/about/news-releases/2023-news-releases/864-board-of-regents-announces-2023-fall-semester-enrollment.

3. At the time of writing, the latest rankings from the National Science Foundation placed WSU as number eight in total engineering research and development from all funding sources and number one specifically in aerospace research and development from all funding sources. See National Center for Science and Engineering Statistics, "Higher Education Research and Development (HERD) Survey," 2024, https://ncses.nsf.gov/surveys/higher-education-research-development/2023.

4. Throughout this book, you will see the names Shocker, Shocker Nation, and other similar references. The names honor the heritage of Wichita State University, originating from its early days as Fairmount College. At that time, some students earned money by "shocking" wheat—harvesting it in nearby fields. Our mascot is named WuShock, who is made of wheat. More on this in chapter 5.

5. I had served as acting president of WSU previously for six months, following the passing of our thirteenth president, and served as interim president for nine months beginning in September 2020.

6. I had the honor of being the first PA to serve as the president of a university. See Steven Lane, "Muma Becomes First PA to Serve as University President," PA Education Association, May 11, 2021, https://paeaonline.org/resources/public-resources/paea-news/muma-becomes-first-pa-to-serve-as-university-president.

## CHAPTER 1. WHO IS WICHITA STATE UNIVERSITY?

1. This focus, which is reflected in the subtitle of this book, is central to WSU, as is apparent on the university's website (wichita.edu).

2. Adam McCann, "Most Diverse Cities in the U.S. (2024)," WalletHub, Apr. 15, 2024, https://wallethub.com/edu/most-diverse-cities/12 690.

3. "WSU Strategic Plan," Wichita State University, 2023, 2024, https://www.wichita.edu/about/strategic_plan/index.php.

4. Roscoe Huhn Eckelberry, *The History of the Municipal University in the United States*, Bulletin, 1932, No. 2, ERIC, accessed Nov. 26, 2024, https://eric.ed.gov/?id=ED542180; *Britannica* (2024), under "Wichita State University," https://www.britannica.com/topic/Wichita-State-University.

5. "Public Institutions," Kansas Board of Regents, 2024, https://www.kansasregents.org/universities_colleges/public-institutions/public_institutions_accessible_list. Washburn University is a municipal university of the city of Topeka, Kansas.

6. WSU Tech is the more commonly known name for Wichita State University Campus of Applied Sciences and Technology, which is a public technical college affiliated with Wichita State University.

7. WSU Strategic Communications, "Wichita State's Record-Breaking Enrollment Driven by Access and Affordability," Wichita State University, Oct. 2, 2024, https://www.wichita.edu/about/wsunews/news/2024/10-oct/2024enrollment_1.php.

8. From Wichita State University's Office of Planning and Analysis.

9. From Wichita State University's Office of Planning and Analysis.

10. WSU Strategic Communications, "Wichita State's Record-Breaking Enrollment Driven by Access and Affordability."

11. "Emerging Hispanic-Serving Institutions (eHSIs): 2022–23," Excelencia in Education, Mar. 2024, https://www.edexcelencia.org/re search/series/emerging-hispanic-serving-institutions.

12. WSU Strategic Communications, "Wichita State's Record-Breaking Enrollment Driven by Access and Affordability."

13. I will discuss each of these in further depth later in this book.

14. John Rydjord, *A History of Fairmount College* (Regents Press of Kansas, 1977).

15. "Wichita State University Announces Death of John Bardo, WCU Chancellor from 1995–2011," Western Carolina University, Mar. 13, 2019, https://www.wcu.edu/stories/posts/News/2019/03/wichita -state-university-announces-death-of-john-bardo-wcu-chancellor -from-1995-2011/index.aspx.

16. John Bardo, "Innovation in the Heartland," *Issues in Science and Technology* 35, no. 2 (2019), https://issues.org/innovation-in-the -heartland/.

17. Bardo, "Innovation in the Heartland."

18. Bardo, "Innovation in the Heartland."

19. Paul Suellentrop, "Closing Braeburn Golf Course Ends an Era for Many Wichita Golfers," *The Wichita Eagle*, Aug. 20, 2014, https://www .kansas.com/news/article1258778.html.

20. Blaine Knott, "Save Braeburn," letter to the editor, *The Wichita Eagle*, Aug. 28, 2014, https://www.kansas.com/opinion/letters-to-the-editor /article1320228.html.

21. Bobby Gandu, correspondence with Sara Tank Ornelas, Dec. 11, 2024.

22. Kimberly Engber, email to Sara Tank Ornelas, Sept. 30, 2024.

23. "Behind the Walls: Lindquist Hall," *The Sunflower*, Apr. 16, 2014, https://thesunflower.com/6099/news/behind-the-walls-lindquist-hall/.

24. Kimberly Engber, email to Sara Tank Ornelas, Sept. 30, 2024.

25. "Wichita State University Honors College Charter," Wichita State University, Dec. 2, 2014, https://www.wichita.edu/academics/honors_col lege/documents/college_charter.pdf.

26. WSU Strategic Communications, "Wichita State's Record-Breaking Enrollment Driven by Access and Affordability."

## CHAPTER 2. A BOLD VISION, A SHARED VISION

1. Beccy Tanner, "WSU President Don Beggs to Retire at the End of June," *The Wichita Eagle*, Sept. 27, 2011, https://www.kansas.com/news /local/article1071129.html.

2. See note 3 in the preface. National Center for Science and Engineering Statistics, "Higher Education Research and Development (HERD) Survey," 2023, https://ncses.nsf.gov/surveys/higher-education -research-development/2022.

3. National Institute for Aviation Research, "About," Wichita State University, accessed Apr. 2, 2025, https://www.wichita.edu/industry _and_defense/NIAR/about-us.php.

4. "Wichita State University Announces Death of John Bardo."

5. Zach Gearhart, interview by Sara Tank Ornelas, June 27, 2023.

6. R. Fisher, W. L. Ury, and B. Patton, *Getting to Yes: Negotiating Agreement Without Giving In* (Penguin Publishing Group, 2011).

7. Lou Heldman, interview by Sara Tank Ornelas and Shelly Coleman-Martins, Dec. 7, 2023.

8. Cindy Claycomb, interview by Sara Tank Ornelas and Shelly Coleman-Martins, Dec. 15, 2023.

9. "2012 Strategic Planning Retreat," Wichita State University, 2012, https://www.wichita.edu/about/strategic_plan/retreat_categories/index .php.

10. Cindy Claycomb, interview by Sara Tank Ornelas and Shelly Coleman-Martins, Dec. 15, 2023.

11. Included are the City of Wichita, Wichita Regional Chamber of Commerce, Wichita Downtown Development Corporation, Regional Economic Area Partnership, and Sedgwick County.

12. "Regional Growth Plan: An Economic Strategy for the Greater Wichita Region," Greater Wichita Partnership, Nov. 2018, https://greaterwichitapartnership.org/user/file/Regional%20Growth%20Plan%20Exec%20Summary_12.12.18.pdf.

13. James Chung, "The Four Challenges: How a City Is Made. Or Broken," The Chung Report, July 28, 2016, https://thechungreport.com/the-four-challenges/.

14. "Wichita State University Strategic Plan," Strategic Planning Steering Committee, Wichita State University, 2013, http://hdl.handle.net/10057/13046.

15. George Dehner, interview by Sara Tank Ornelas, Aug. 3, 2023.

16. Jay Price, interview by Sara Tank Ornelas, July 31, 2023.

17. Amy Drassen Ham, interview by Sara Tank Ornelas, Nov. 3, 2023.

18. Cindy Claycomb, interview by Sara Tank Ornelas and Shelly Coleman-Martins, Dec. 15, 2023.

19. Leslie Garren, "Strategic Planning Artifact," Appendix A, p. 20, Wichita State University, Apr. 30, 2013, https://www.wichita.edu/about/strategic_plan/documents/Artifact_Primary_Data_Process_Print.pdf.

20. "Whose University Is It Anyway?," paid political advertisement, The Wichita Eagle, Apr. 15, 2018.

21. "Innovative Thinking for Today's Realities in Higher Education," paid political advertisement, The Wichita Eagle, Apr. 22, 2018.

22. Jenna Farhat and Chance Swaim, "Students Stage Sit-In Protest at President Bardo's Office," The Sunflower, Mar. 14, 2017, https://thesunflower.com/15818/news/students-protest-sit-in-outside-president-bardos-office/.

23. Jenna Farhat et al., "SGA Passes Vote of No Confidence in President Bardo," The Sunflower, Mar. 16, 2017, https://thesunflower.com/15874/news/sga-passes-vote-of-no-confidence-in-president-bardo/.

24. Jan Twomey, interview by Sara Tank Ornelas, Nov. 9, 2023.

25. Evan Pflugradt, "President John Bardo Discusses Shared Governance, Campus Changes," The Sunflower, Apr. 27, 2017, https://thesunflower.com/17548/news/president-john-bardo-discusses-shared-governance-campus-changes/.

26. Lou Heldman, interview by Sara Tank Ornelas and Shelly Coleman-Martins, Dec. 7, 2023.

## CHAPTER 3. LEAN INTO POSSIBILITY

1. "Wichita State University Becoming an Innovation-Focused University," *Newswise*, Aug. 20, 2014, https://www.newswise.com/articles/wichita-state-university-becoming-an-innovation-focused-university.

2. Wichita Area Technical College affiliated with WSU in 2018 as an innovative solution to build workforce utilizing the GED to the PhD. It is now known as the Wichita State University Campus of Applied Sciences and Technology and is doing business as WSU Tech.

3. Sheree Utash, interview by Sara Tank Ornelas and Shelly Coleman-Martins, July 26, 2023.

4. Bardo, "Innovation in the Heartland."

5. Rob Gerlach, interview by Sara Tank Ornelas, Aug. 24, 2023.

6. Formerly known as Counseling and Prevention Services, it was rebranded after the launch of its Health, Outreach, Prevention and Education (HOPE) Services program in 2023.

7. "Suspenders4Hope," Wichita State University, accessed Mar. 7, 2024, https://suspenders4hope.com/.

8. Rob Gerlach, interview by Sara Tank Ornelas, Aug. 24, 2023.

9. These partners include Ascension Via Christi, Wichita-based Thrive Restaurant Group, Nebraska Wesleyan University, and Penn State Altoona, among others. See Abigail Klein, "Wichita State Preventing Suicide Program Provides Crucial Support for Local Businesses," Wichita State University, Sept. 12, 2022, https://www.wichita.edu/about/wsunews/news/2022/09-sept/PreventingSuicide_7.php.

10. Rob Gerlach, interview by Sara Tank Ornelas, Aug. 24, 2023.

11. Cheyla Clawson, interview by Sara Tank Ornelas, Nov. 6, 2023.

12. "Wichita State University," Carnegie Classification of Institutions of Higher Education, accessed Mar. 31, 2025, https://carnegieclassifications.acenet.edu/institution/wichita-state-university/.

13. Beech is the namesake of Wichita-based Beechcraft, a Textron company.

14. Shirley Lefever, interview by Sara Tank Ornelas, Aug. 8, 2023.

15. United States Census Bureau, "Annual Estimates of the Resident Population for Incorporated Places in Kansas: April 1, 2020 to July 1, 2022," 2023.

16. Shirley Lefever, interview by Sara Tank Ornelas, Aug. 8, 2023.

17. John Tomblin, interview by Sara Tank Ornelas, July 7, 2023.

18. National Center for Science and Engineering Statistics, "Higher Education Research and Development (HERD) Survey."

19. National Center for Science and Engineering Statistics, "Higher Education Research and Development (HERD) Survey."

20. National Center for Science and Engineering Statistics, "Higher Education Research and Development (HERD) Survey."

21. National Center for Science and Engineering Statistics, "Higher Education Research and Development (HERD) Survey."

22. WSU Strategic Communications, "WSU Awarded $51 Million to Advance Smart Manufacturing in South Kansas," news release, Wichita State University, Sept. 2, 2022, https://www.wichita.edu/about/wsunews -releases/2022/08-aug/build_back_better_award_4.php.

23. WSU Strategic Communications, "NIAR Engages Federal Grants to Accelerate Growth of Advanced Materials and Manufacturing," news release, Wichita State University, Oct. 18, 2023, https://www.wichita .edu/about/wsunews-releases/2023/10-oct/advanced_manufacturing _release_3.php.

24. Titus Wu, "Kansas' COVID-19 Testing Capacity Finally Seeing a Boost," *The Topeka Capital-Journal*, Dec. 31, 2020, https://www.cjonline .com/story/news/coronavirus/2020/12/31/kansas-covid-19-testing -capacity-finally-seeing-boost/4065409001/.

25. Sara Tank Ornelas, "Wichita State Celebrates Opening of High-Volume COVID-19 Test Lab," Wichita State University, Oct. 19, 2020, https://www.wichita.edu/about/wsunews/news/2020/10-oct/MDL opening_9.php.

26. From Wichita State's Molecular Diagnostics Laboratory.

## CHAPTER 4. MANIFEST THE VISION

1. Wichita State University's Innovation Campus was designated the 2023 Emerging Research Park by the Association of University Research Parks.

2. Suellentrop, "Closing Braeburn Golf Course Ends an Era for Many Wichita Golfers."

3. "Wichita State University Becoming an Innovation-Focused University."

4. Beccy Tanner, "Grand Opening of Wichita State's Swanky Shocker Hall Marks a New Era," *The Wichita Eagle*, June 16, 2015, https://www.kansas.com/news/local/education/article1226167.html.

5. "Wichita State University Becoming an Innovation-Focused University." Some readers may recognize the name Braeburn from WSU's current Braeburn Square—located on the Innovation Campus and on the former site of the Braeburn Golf Course—which is a mixed-use space that offers retail, service, and restaurant businesses a chance to set up shop on campus and for the surrounding community.

6. Bob Lutz, "WSU Takes a Swing at Innovation While Closing Braeburn Golf Course," *The Wichita Eagle*, Aug. 20, 2014, https://www.kansas.com/sports/spt-columns-blogs/bob-lutz/article1258360.html.

7. Jay Price, interview by Sara Tank Ornelas, July 31, 2023. After the trees were removed from the Innovation Campus, many more were planted elsewhere on campus.

8. Gery Markova, interview by Sara Tank Ornelas, Nov. 3, 2023.

9. Mark Vermillion, interview by Sara Tank Ornelas, Nov. 6, 2023.

10. Chance Swaim, "Faculty Senate Letter Confirmed, Sent to President Bardo," *The Sunflower*, Mar. 16, 2017, https://thesunflower.com/15882/news/faculty-senate-letter-confirmed-sent-to-president-bardo/.

11. Swaim, "Faculty Senate Letter Confirmed."

12. Andy Schlapp, interview by Sara Tank Ornelas, June 26, 2023.

13. Suzanne Perez Tobias, "WSU Defends Koch-Funded Private School Being Built on Campus," *The Wichita Eagle*, Feb. 7, 2018, https://www.kansas.com/news/local/education/article198704414.html.

14. Dan Voorhis, "Wichita State's New Engineering Building Opens on Innovation Campus," *The Wichita Eagle*, Jan. 18, 2017, https://www.kansas.com/news/business/article127344084.html.

15. WSU Strategic Communications, "Experiential Engineering Building Will Be Renamed John Bardo Center," news release, June 19, 2019, https://www.wichita.edu/about/wsunews-releases/2019/06-jun/bardo_center_release.php.

16. Jerry Siebenmark, "Airbus' Move to WSU Campus Brings Benefits Beyond New Building," *The Wichita Eagle*, Jan. 4, 2017, https://www.kansas.com/news/business/aviation/article124603509.html.

17. John Tomblin, interview by Sara Tank Ornelas, July 7, 2023.

18. Kevin White, "WSU Announces Airbus to Build on Innovation Campus," KSNW-TV, Mar. 24, 2015, https://www.ksn.com/news/wsu-announces-airbus-to-build-on-innovation-campus/.

19. Tracee Friess, interview by Sara Tank Ornelas, July 7, 2023.

20. "Wichita State University," Graduate Criminal Justice Program Overview, *U.S. News and World Report*. Accessed Dec. 10, 2024. https://www.usnews.com.

21. John Tomblin, interview by Sara Tank Ornelas, July 7, 2023.

22. "Crime Gun Intelligence Center," City of Wichita, 2024, https://www.wichita.gov/880/Crime-Gun-Intelligence-Center.

23. Bureau of Alcohol, Tobacco, Firearms and Explosives, "ATF Announces Crime Gun Intelligence Center of Excellence," US Department of Justice, June 29, 2022, https://www.atf.gov/news/press-releases/atf-announces-crime-gun-intelligence-center-excellence.

24. Larisa Genin, interview by Sara Tank Ornelas, Sept. 23, 2024.

25. Larisa Genin, interview by Sara Tank Ornelas, Sept. 23, 2024.

26. Larisa Genin, interview by Sara Tank Ornelas, Sept. 23, 2024.

27. "Wichita State Innovation Campus Aims to Unite University and Community," *Silicon Prairie News*, Jan. 5, 2016, https://siliconprairienews.com/2016/01/wichita-state-innovation-campus-aims-to-unite-university-and-community/.

28. Zach Gearhart, interview by Sara Tank Ornelas, June 27, 2023.

## CHAPTER 5. EMBRACE YOUR IDENTITY

1. United States Census Bureau, "Annual Estimates of the Resident Population for Incorporated Places in Kansas: April 1, 2020 to July 1, 2022," 2023.

2. As noted by McCann, "Most Diverse Cities in the U.S. (2024)," which sourced information from the US Census Bureau and the US Religion Census.

3. "Data Insight: Points of Pride," Greater Wichita Partnership, 2022, accessed Apr. 1, 2025, https://greaterwichitapartnership.org//user/file /greater-wichita-region-accolades-2022.pdf. Also United States Census Bureau, "QuickFacts: Wichita City, Kansas," July 1, 2024, https://www .census.gov/quickfacts/fact/table/wichitacitykansas/PST045224.

4. City of Wichita, "Aerospace," accessed Apr. 1, 2025, https://www .wichita.gov/269/Aerospace.

5. Angela Tague, "10 Best Metros for First-Time Home Buyers," Zillow, Feb. 2, 2023, https://www.zillow.com/learn/best-cities-for-first -time-home-buyers/.

6. As reported in 2012, 17.8 percent of all jobs in Wichita were in manufacturing, the highest among major metropolitan areas, and 64.1 percent of the city's manufacturing jobs were labeled as "very high-tech," behind only San Jose, California, and Palm Bay, Florida. See Howard Wial, "Interactive: Locating American Manufacturing," Brookings, May 9, 2012, https://www.brookings.edu/articles/interactive-locating -american-manufacturing/.

7. The airport is served by Alaska Airlines, Allegiant Air, American Airlines, Delta Air Lines, Southwest Airlines, and United Airlines. See "Airline Information," Wichita Dwight D. Eisenhower National Airport, accessed Mar. 8, 2024, https://www.flywichita.com/airline-information/.

8. This includes clear to partly cloudy days, as defined by the National Oceanic and Atmospheric Administration. See "Comparative Climatic Data," National Oceanic and Atmospheric Administration, 2018, https://www.ncei.noaa.gov/products/land-based-station/comparative -climatic-data.

9. Adam McCann, "Best Summer Travel Destinations," Wallet Hub, May 14, 2023, https://wallethub.com/edu/best-summer-travel-des tinations/3792.

10. Oresmus Hills Bentley, ed., *History of Wichita and Sedgwick County, Kansas, Past and Present, Including an Account of the Cities, Towns and Villages of the County* (C. F. Cooper and Co., 1910), https:// archive.org/details/historyofwichita01bent/.

11. "Chamber History," Wichita Regional Chamber of Commerce, accessed Dec. 9, 2024, https://www.wichitachamber.org/aboutchamber /chamber-history/.

12. The Aeronautical Chamber of Commerce of America, now the Aerospace Industries Association, declared Wichita the "Air Capital City" of America in the early 1900s, a name that Wichita has embraced and taken to new levels to declare itself the Air Capital of the World. See David Freed, "We Built This City," *Smithsonian Magazine*, Sept. 2018, https://www.smithsonianmag.com/air-space-magazine/04_sep2018 -spirit-of-wichita-1-180969914/.

13. "Aerospace Overview," Greater Wichita Partnership, accessed Dec. 10, 2024, https://greaterwichitapartnership.org/industry-selectors /aerospace/overview.

14. James Chung, "The Entrepreneurship Challenge: More Than a Buzzword," The Chung Report, July 28, 2016, https://thechungreport .com/the-entrepreneurship-challenge/.

15. Craig Miner, *Uncloistered Halls: The Centennial History of Wichita State University* (Wichita State University, Endowment Association, 1995). Vassar is short for Vassar Female College, now just Vassar College. Before Fairmount College came to be, the original vision was to create a women's college in Wichita—called by many names, including Young Ladies' College, Wichita Ladies' College, and Congregational Female College—which later became the Fairmount Institute and finally Fairmount College. See Rydjord, *History of Fairmount College.*

16. The manager Roy Kirk was believed to be the one who first sug- gested the name. See Rydjord, *History of Fairmount College.*

17. The full name of the university was the Municipal University of Wichita, which was often referred to as just Wichita University.

18. "WuShock: A True Original," Wichita State University, accessed Apr. 2, 2025, https://www.wichita.edu/about/wushock.php.

19. Lou Heldman, interview by Sara Tank Ornelas and Shelly Coleman-Martins, Dec. 7, 2023.

20. Jeff Fluhr, interview by Shelly Coleman-Martins, Mar. 13, 2025.

21. Zach Gearhart, interview by Sara Tank Ornelas, June 29, 2023.

22. John Bardo, "Renewing Wichita's Promise: The University, the City, the Region and Economic Development," Wichita State University, 2018, https://www.wichita.edu/administration/president/documents/ecodev5.pdf.

23. Shirley Lefever, interview by Sara Tank Ornelas, Aug. 8, 2023.

24. WSU News Services, "New Online Teacher Apprentice Program Will Help Curb Teacher Shortage," Wichita State University, July 5, 2017, https://www.wichita.edu/about/wsunews/archive/index.php?nid=3662.

25. Jennifer Lane, "WSU Teacher Apprentice Program Has Positive Impact on Kansas Economy," Wichita State University, Nov. 10, 2021, https://www.wichita.edu/academics/applied_studies/News/tap-economic-impact.php.

26. Lane, "WSU Teacher Apprentice Program Has Positive Impact."

27. Lane, "WSU Teacher Apprentice Program Has Positive Impact."

28. Jill Wood, email to Sara Tank Ornelas, Apr. 13, 2023.

29. Marcus Clem, "How a Wichita State Program Could Help Solve Kansas' Teacher Shortage," *The Beacon*, Aug. 22, 2024, https://thebeaconnews.org/stories/2024/08/22/teacher-apprenticeship-program-could-help-solve-kansas-shortage/.

30. "Retired B-1B Arrives in Wichita to Create a Digital Twin," McConnell Air Force Base, Mar. 27, 2025, https://www.mcconnell.af.mil/News/Article/3659646/retired-b-1b-arrives-in-wichita-to-create-a-digital-twin/.

31. WSU Strategic Communications, "NIAR Announces New Partnerships for Boeing 777 Conversion Program," Wichita State University, Sept. 29, 2020, https://www.wichita.edu/about/wsunews-releases/2020/09-sept/boeing_777_conversion_9.php.

32. Sara Tank Ornelas, "Wichita State Professor Wins Innovation

Award to Create Accessible Comic Book App," Wichita State University, Feb. 3, 2021, https://www.wichita.edu/about/wsunews/news/2021/02 -feb/vizling_3.php.

33. Sara Tank Ornelas, "Wichita State Researchers Aim to Educate, Protect Refugees from Cyber-Scams," Wichita State University, June 20, 2022, https://www.wichita.edu/about/wsunews/news/2022/06-jun /refugees_3.php.

34. Sara Tank Ornelas, "WSU Researchers Win $1.4 Million NSF Grant to Mitigate Environmental Impact of Road Salt," Wichita State University, Sept. 15, 2022, https://www.wichita.edu/about/wsunews /news/2022/09-sept/roadsalt_3.php.

35. Sara Tank Ornelas, "Treatment for Burn Wounds Could Be Revolutionized Through Wichita State Research," Wichita State University, Feb. 8, 2023, https://www.wichita.edu/about/wsunews/news/2023/02 -feb/burnwound_3.php.

36. Shirley Lefever, interview by Sara Tank Ornelas, Aug. 8, 2023.

37. WSU News, "Wichita State Accepts Invitation to Join American Athletic Conference," Wichita State University, Apr. 7, 2017, https://www .wichita.edu/about/wsunews/news/2017/04-april/wsu_joins_aac.php.

## CHAPTER 6. WHO DO YOU SERVE?

1. State Higher Education Executive Officers Association, "State Higher Education Finance Report: FY 2023," State Higher Education Finance, 2024, https://shef.sheeo.org/report/.

2. Andy Schlapp, interview by Sara Tank Ornelas, June 26, 2023.

3. Gery Markova, interview by Sara Tank Ornelas, Nov. 3, 2023.

4. United States Census Bureau, "Historical Population Change Data (1910–2020)," Apr. 26, 2021, https://www.census.gov/data/tables/time -series/dec/popchange-data-text.html.

5. Roy Wenzl, "New Wichita State Scholarship Program Aims to Boost Enrollment," *The Wichita Eagle*, Aug. 6, 2014, https://www.kansas .com/article1125336.html.

6. Roy Wenzl, "Wichita State Hires Recruiting Firm to Boost En-

rollment," *The Wichita Eagle*, Aug. 6, 2014, https://www.kansas.com/news /article1123568.html.

7. Shirley Lefever, interview by Sara Tank Ornelas, Aug. 8, 2023.

8. Ashlie Jack, interview by Sara Tank Ornelas, Apr. 2, 2025.

9. Carolyn Shaw, "SEM Update—Oct. 22, 2021," Wichita State University, 2021, https://www.wichita.edu/academics/academic_affairs/SEM /sem_oct_21.php.

10. When comparing 2016 enrollment with 2020 enrollment. See Elaine Frisbie, "Enrollment Report," Kansas Board of Regents, Mar. 16, 2022, https://www.kansasregents.org/resources/PDF/Enrollment_Report _2022_FINAL.pdf.

11. Carolyn Shaw, interview by Sara Tank Ornelas, July 31, 2023.

12. John Bardo, "John Bardo: I-35 Corridor a Key to Growing Economy," opinion, *The Wichita Eagle*, June 26, 2016, https://www.kansas .com/opinion/opn-columns-blogs/article85895672.html.

13. "Shocker City Partnership," Wichita State University, 2024, https://www.wichita.edu/services/accounts_receivable/ar_shocker_city _partnership.php.

14. "Shocker Select Tuition Discount," Wichita State University, 2024, https://www.wichita.edu/admissions/undergraduate/tuition_programs /shocker_select.php.

15. Bardo, "John Bardo: I-35 Corridor a Key to Growing Economy."

16. See "Student Enrollment Factbook for Fall Census Day," table 12, Wichita State University, 2023, https://www.wichita.edu/services /planning_and_analysis/documents/Enrollment_Fall_Census_OPA web.pdf.

17. "Kansas Higher Education Statistics," Kansas Board of Regents, 2024, https://kansasregents.org/data/system_data/enrollment_reports.

18. "Kansas Higher Education Statistics."

## CHAPTER 7. BEYOND BEING AN EMPLOYER, DRIVING PROSPERITY

1. Bardo, "Innovation in the Heartland."

2. George Dehner, interview by Sara Tank Ornelas, Aug. 3, 2023.

3. "Glossary of Terms," Wichita State University, 2024, https://www
.wichita.edu/academics/applied_learning/applied-learning-model
/glossary.php.

4. Paul Suellentrop, "Wichita State Students Benefit from Applied
Learning at Help Hangar," Wichita State University, Mar. 16, 2019, https://
www.wichita.edu/about/wsunews/news/2019/03-march/helphang
ar.php.

5. Sara Tank Ornelas, "Engineers Without Borders Building Much-
Needed Bridge for Ecuadorian Village," Wichita State University, Aug. 28,
2023, https://www.wichita.edu/about/wsunews/news/2023/08-aug/ewb
_2.php.

6. Paul Suellentrop, "Wichita State Helps NASA Evaluate Possibilities for Life on Other Planets," Wichita State University, May 17, 2023,
https://www.wichita.edu/about/wsunews/news/2023/05-may/microbes
_3.php; Caelin Bragg, "Wichita State Professor and Student Earn NASA
Grant to Explore Harmful Cosmic Radiation," Wichita State University,
May 7, 2024, https://www.wichita.edu/about/wsunews/news/2024/05
-may/nasa-grant_3.php; Paul Suellentrop, "Wichita State Is Now Home
to a Nanosatellite, Taking Research on NASA Project to a New Level,"
Wichita State University, July 11, 2024, https://www.wichita.edu/about
/wsunews/news/2024/07-july/cubesat_3.php.

7. Sara Tank Ornelas, "WSU's Gateway to IP Program Leads STEM
Students into Patent Law Careers," Wichita State University, May 3, 2023,
https://www.wichita.edu/about/wsunews/news/2023/05-may/gate
way_2.php.

8. Sara Tank Ornelas, "WSU Lab That Took Off During COVID
Switches Gears to Microbiology," Wichita State University, Apr. 6, 2023,
https://www.wichita.edu/about/wsunews/news/2023/04-april/MDL
BeyondCovid_3.php.

9. Sara Tank Ornelas, "Wichita State Archaeologists Dig In to Unearth Cultural History," Wichita State University, Nov. 8, 2021, https://
www.wichita.edu/about/wsunews/news/2021/11-nov/cityarchaeologist
_3.php.

10. Sara Tank Ornelas, "Digital Twin Program Brings New Life to

Old Aircraft," Wichita State University, July 8, 2020, https://www.wichita
.edu/about/wsunews/news/2020/07-july/digital-twin_9.php; WSU Strategic Communications, "Air Force to Develop F-16 'Digital Twin' with
Help from Wichita State NIAR," Wichita State University, June 30,
2021, https://www.wichita.edu/about/wsunews/news/2021/06-jun/f-16
_3.php; "WSU to Help Modernize and Replace USAF's 'Nightwatch'
Presidential Emergency Command Center Aircraft Fleet," Wichita State
University, Dec. 3, 2024, https://www.wichita.edu/about/wsunews/news
/2024/12-dec/nightwatch_story_3.php.

11. Amy Drassen Ham, interview by Sara Tank Ornelas, Nov. 3, 2023.

12. Bobby Gandu, correspondence with Sara Tank Ornelas, Dec. 11,
2024.

13. Bobby Gandu, correspondence with Sara Tank Ornelas, Dec. 11,
2024.

14. Thousands of Shockers earned over $30 million in fiscal year
2022–2023. See "Shocker Career Accelerator Annual Report 2022–2023,"
Wichita State University, 2024, https://my.visme.co/v/764rgd9z-yvqmjg.

15. See "Student Enrollment Factbook for Fall Census Day," table 9.

16. Teri Hall, correspondence with Sara Tank Ornelas, Mar. 14, 2024.

17. Teri Hall, correspondence with Sara Tank Ornelas, Mar. 14, 2024.

18. Tonya Witherspoon, interview by Sara Tank Ornelas, June 28,
2023.

19. Abigail Klein, "Beyond the Classroom: Keegan Staats," Wichita
State University, May 25, 2022, https://www.wichita.edu/about/wsunews
/news/2022/05-may/Keegan_2.php.

20. Tracee Friess, "NSF Director Praises 'Amazing' Applied Learning at Wichita State," Wichita State University, Jan. 25, 2023, https://
www.wichita.edu/about/wsunews/news/2023/01-jan/NSFdirectorvisit
_4.php.

21. Sara Tank Ornelas, "Beyond the Classroom: Alia Michaelis,"
Wichita State University, May 23, 2022, https://www.wichita.edu/about
/wsunews/news/2022/05-may/michaelis_2.php.

22. "Wichita State Innovation Partner: Deloitte's Smart Factory @

Wichita," Wichita State University, Mar. 13, 2023, https://www.wichita
.edu/about/wsunews/news/2023/03-march/smartfactory_4.php.

**CHAPTER 8. WHAT'S IN IT FOR EVERYONE?**

1. Suzanne Perez Tobias, "Wichita State, WATC Discussing Possible Expanded Affiliation or Merger," *The Wichita Eagle*, Oct. 21, 2015, https://www.kansas.com/news/local/education/article40529304.html.

2. Daniel Salazar, "Bill Would Allow Technical College to Merge with Wichita State," *The Wichita Eagle*, Feb. 27, 2016, https://www.kansas.com/news/local/education/article62875372.html.

3. Sheree Utash, interview by Sara Tank Ornelas and Shelly Coleman-Martins, July 26, 2023.

4. Sheree Utash, interview by Sara Tank Ornelas and Shelly Coleman-Martins, July 26, 2023.

5. Matthew Kelly and Ray Strunk, "WSU Finalizes Merger with WATC, Will Move Closer to Enrollment Goal," *The Sunflower*, Nov. 16, 2017, https://thesunflower.com/22442/news/wsu-finalizes-merger-with-watc-will-move-closer-to-enrollment-goal/.

6. "WSU Topics: Get to Know WSU Tech," Wichita State University, last updated May 2, 2019, https://www.wichita.edu/about/public_information/wsu_topics/topics_wsu_tech.php.

7. "Programs of Study," WSU Tech, 2024, https://wsutech.edu/admissions/programs-of-study/.

8. John Tomblin, interview by Sara Tank Ornelas, July 7, 2023.

9. "Non-Discrimination," WSU Tech, 2024, https://wsutech.edu/nondiscrimination/.

10. Sheree Utash, interview by Sara Tank Ornelas and Shelly Coleman-Martins, July 26, 2023.

11. Bill Roy, host, "Sheree Utash, Wichita Area Technical College," *BizTalk*, podcast audio, Nov. 10, 2017, https://soundcloud.com/biztalkwiththewbj/episode-24-sheree-utash-wichita-area-technical-college.

12. Sheree Utash, "It's Official: WATC Will Become the WSU Campus of Applied Sciences and Technology," news release, WSU Tech, accessed Dec. 12, 2024, https://wsutech.edu/archived/official-watc-will-become -wsu-campus-applied-sciences-technology/.

13. WSU Strategic Communications, "New Wichita State Partnership with WSU Tech and Butler Will Help Critical Teacher Shortage," Wichita State University, July 5, 2023, https://www.wichita.edu/about/wsunews /news/2023/07-july/cas_pathway_2.php.

14. "Wichita Biomedical Campus," Wichita State University, May 8, 2024, https://www.wichita.edu/academics/wichita_biomedical_campus /index.php.

15. Zach Gearhart, interview by Sara Tank Ornelas, June 27, 2023.

16. Joyce Martin et al., "Births: Final Data for 2007," Centers for Disease Control, *National Vital Statistics Reports* 58, no. 24 (Aug. 9, 2010): 1–85; Michelle Osterman et al., "Births: Final Data for 2022," Centers for Disease Control, *National Vital Statistics Reports* 73, no. 2 (Apr. 2024): 1–56.

17. "Immediate College Enrollment Rate," National Center for Education Statistics, May 2024, https://nces.ed.gov/programs/coe/indicator /cpa/immediate-college-enrollment-rate.

18. "Immediate College Enrollment Rate."

19. University Faculty Senate, "Minutes from the General Faculty Meeting," Wichita State University, May 5, 2017, https://www.wichita .edu/academics/facultysenate/Mgenfac5517.php.

20. Jordan Walker, "Quality education doesn't have to mean a traditional four year degree," Facebook, Mar. 30, 2017, https://www.face book.com/share/p/1GFvEra75j/.

21. Charles Ogden: "I think this is a fantastic opportunity for students following a skilled-trades path," Facebook, Mar. 30, 2017, https://www.face book.com/share/1Dw8e7mVgQ/.

## CHAPTER 9. EVERYTHING COMES DOWN TO PRIORITIES

1. "WSU Strategic Plan."

2. "Building a Future," in *Strategic Plan for Kansas*, Kansas Board of Regents, 2020, https://www.kansasregents.org/about/building-a-future.

3. We developed WSU's Student Success and Persistence initiative, which closely aligns with the Kansas Board of Regents' National Institute for Student Success, and just recently, we opened the Shocker Success Center, offering a centralized location for numerous student support services in the heart of our campus.

4. Ashley Mowreader, "Report: Cost of College, Stress Pushes Students to Consider Stopping Out," *Inside Higher Ed*, Apr. 18, 2024, https://www.insidehighered.com/news/student-success/health-wellness/2024/04/18/why-college-students-drop-out-school-and-what-can.

5. "States That Offer the Most Need-Based Scholarships and Grants," Scholaroo, Aug. 28, 2023, https://scholaroo.com/report/scholarships-and-grants-rankings/.

6. WSU Strategic Communications, "Wichita State's Record-Breaking Enrollment Driven by Access and Affordability."

7. George Dehner, interview by Sara Tank Ornelas, Aug. 3, 2023.

8. Ashley Mowreader, "Survey: Why Students Enroll and Why They Persist," *Inside Higher Ed*, Feb. 23, 2024, https://www.insidehighered.com/news/student-success/academic-life/2024/02/23/student-survey-gauges-importance-college-degree.

# References

· · · · · · · · · · · · · · · · · · · · · · · · · · · · · · · · · · · · · · · · · · · · · · · ·

"Aerospace Overview." Greater Wichita Partnership. Accessed Dec. 10, 2024. https://greaterwichitapartnership.org/industry-selectors /aerospace/overview.

"Airline Information." Wichita Dwight D. Eisenhower National Airport. Accessed Mar. 8, 2024. https://www.flywichita.com/airline -information/.

Bardo, John. "Innovation in the Heartland." *Issues in Science and Technology* 35, no. 2 (2019). https://issues.org/innovation-in-the-heartland/.

———. "John Bardo: I-35 Corridor a Key to Growing Economy." Opinion, *The Wichita Eagle*, June 26, 2016. https://www.kansas.com /opinion/opn-columns-blogs/article85895672.html.

———. "Renewing Wichita's Promise: The University, the City, the Region and Economic Development." Wichita State University, 2018. https://www.wichita.edu/administration/president/documents /ecodev5.pdf.

"Behind the Walls: Lindquist Hall." *The Sunflower*, Apr. 16, 2014. https:// thesunflower.com/6099/news/behind-the-walls-lindquist-hall/.

Bentley, Oresmus Hills, ed. *History of Wichita and Sedgwick County, Kansas: Past and Present, Including an Account of the Cities, Towns and Villages of the County.* C. F. Cooper and Co., 1910. https://archive .org/details/historyofwichita01bent/.

"Board of Regents Announces 2023 Fall Semester Enrollment." News release. Kansas Board of Regents. Sept. 27, 2023. https://www .kansasregents.org/about/news-releases/2023-news-releases/864 -board-of-regents-announces-2023-fall-semester-enrollment.

Bragg, Caelin. "Wichita State Professor and Student Earn NASA Grant to Explore Harmful Cosmic Radiation." Wichita State University. May 7, 2024. https://www.wichita.edu/about/wsunews/news/2024/05-may/nasa-grant_3.php.

"Building a Future." In *Strategic Plan for Kansas*. Kansas Board of Regents. 2020. https://www.kansasregents.org/about/building-a-future.

Bureau of Alcohol, Tobacco, Firearms and Explosives. "ATF Announces Crime Gun Intelligence Center of Excellence." US Department of Justice. June 29, 2022. https://www.atf.gov/news/press-releases/atf-announces-crime-gun-intelligence-center-excellence.

"Chamber History." Wichita Regional Chamber of Commerce. Accessed Dec. 9, 2024. https://www.wichitachamber.org/aboutchamber/chamber-history/.

Chung, James. "The Entrepreneurship Challenge: More Than a Buzzword." The Chung Report. July 28, 2016. https://thechungreport.com/the-entrepreneurship-challenge/.

———. "The Four Challenges: How a City Is Made. Or Broken." The Chung Report. July 28, 2016. https://thechungreport.com/the-four-challenges/.

City of Wichita. "Aerospace." Accessed Apr. 1, 2025. https://www.wichita.gov/269/Aerospace.

Clem, Marcus. "How a Wichita State Program Could Help Solve Kansas' Teacher Shortage." *The Beacon*, Aug. 22, 2024. https://thebeaconnews.org/stories/2024/08/22/teacher-apprenticeship-program-could-help-solve-kansas-shortage/.

"Comparative Climatic Data." National Oceanic and Atmospheric Administration. 2018. https://www.ncei.noaa.gov/products/land-based-station/comparative-climatic-data.

"Crime Gun Intelligence Center." City of Wichita. 2024. https://www.wichita.gov/880/Crime-Gun-Intelligence-Center.

"Data Insight: Points of Pride." Greater Wichita Partnership. 2022. Accessed Apr. 1, 2025. https://greaterwichitapartnership.org//user/file/greater-wichita-region-accolades-2022.pdf.

Eckelberry, Roscoe Huhn. *The History of the Municipal University in the United States.* Bulletin, 1932, No. 2. ERIC. Accessed Nov. 26, 2024. https://eric.ed.gov/?id=ED542180.

"Emerging Hispanic-Serving Institutions (eHSIs): 2022–23." Excelencia in Education. Mar. 2024. https://www.edexcelencia.org/research /series/emerging-hispanic-serving-institutions.

Farhat, Jenna, Matthew Kelly, Andrew Linnabary, and Chance Swaim. "SGA Passes Vote of No Confidence in President Bardo." *The Sunflower,* Mar. 16, 2017. https://thesunflower.com/15874/news/sga-pass es-vote-of-no-confidence-in-president-bardo/.

Farhat, Jenna, and Chance Swaim. "Students Stage Sit-In Protest at President Bardo's Office." *The Sunflower,* Mar. 14, 2017. https://the sunflower.com/15818/news/students-protest-sit-in-outside-pres ident-bardos-office/.

Fisher, R., W. L. Ury, and B. Patton. *Getting to Yes: Negotiating Agreement without Giving In.* Penguin Publishing Group, 2011.

Freed, David. "We Built This City." *Smithsonian Magazine,* Sept. 2018. https://www.smithsonianmag.com/air-space-magazine/04_sep2018 -spirit-of-wichita-1-180969914/.

Friess, Tracee. "NSF Director Praises 'Amazing' Applied Learning at Wichita State." Wichita State University. Jan. 25, 2023. https://www .wichita.edu/about/wsunews/news/2023/01-jan/NSFdirectorvisit _4.php.

Frisbie, Elaine. *Enrollment Report.* Kansas Board of Regents. Mar. 16, 2022. https://www.kansasregents.org/resources/PDF/Enrollment_Re port_2022_FINAL.pdf.

Garren, Leslie. "Strategic Planning Artifact." Appendix A, p. 20. Wichita State University. Apr. 30, 2013. https://www.wichita.edu/about /strategic_plan/documents/Artifact_Primary_Data_Process_Print .pdf.

"Glossary of Terms." Wichita State University. 2024. https://www.wichita .edu/academics/applied_learning/applied-learning-model/glossary .php.

"Immediate College Enrollment Rate." National Center for Education Statistics. May 2024. https://nces.ed.gov/programs/coe/indicator/cpa/immediate-college-enrollment-rate.

"Innovative Thinking for Today's Realities in Higher Education." Paid political advertisement. *The Wichita Eagle*, Apr. 22, 2018.

"Kansas Higher Education Statistics." Kansas Board of Regents. 2024. https://kansasregents.org/data/system_data/enrollment_reports.

Kelly, Matthew, and Ray Strunk. "WSU Finalizes Merger with WATC, Will Move Closer to Enrollment Goal." *The Sunflower*, Nov. 16, 2017. https://thesunflower.com/22442/news/wsu-finalizes-merger-with-watc-will-move-closer-to-enrollment-goal/.

Klein, Abigail. "Beyond the Classroom: Keegan Staats." Wichita State University. May 25, 2022. https://www.wichita.edu/about/wsunews/news/2022/05-may/Keegan_2.php.

———. "Wichita State Preventing Suicide Program Provides Crucial Support for Local Businesses." Wichita State University. Sept. 12, 2022. https://www.wichita.edu/about/wsunews/news/2022/09-sept/PreventingSuicide_7.php.

Knott, Blaine. "Save Braeburn." Letter to the editor. *The Wichita Eagle*, Aug. 28, 2014. https://www.kansas.com/opinion/letters-to-the-editor/article1320228.html.

Lane, Jennifer. "WSU Teacher Apprentice Program Has Positive Impact on Kansas Economy." Wichita State University. Nov. 10, 2021. https://www.wichita.edu/academics/applied_studies/News/tap-economic-impact.php.

Lane, Steven. "Muma Becomes First PA to Serve as University President." PA Education Association. May 11, 2021. https://paeaonline.org/resources/public-resources/paea-news/muma-becomes-first-pa-to-serve-as-university-president.

Lutz, Bob. "WSU Takes a Swing at Innovation While Closing Braeburn Golf Course." *The Wichita Eagle*, Aug. 20, 2014. https://www.kansas.com/sports/spt-columns-blogs/bob-lutz/article1258360.html.

Marcus, Jon. "A Looming 'Demographic Cliff': Fewer College Students and Ultimately Fewer Graduates." NPR. Jan. 25, 2025. https://www.npr.org/2025/01/08/nx-s1-5246200/demographic-cliff-fewer-college-students-mean-fewer-graduates.

Martin, Joyce, Brady Hamilton, Paul Sutton, Stephanie Ventura, T. J. Mathews, Sharon Kirmeyer, and Michelle Osterman. "Births: Final Data for 2007." Centers for Disease Control. *National Vital Statistics Report* 58, no. 24 (Aug. 2010).

McCann, Adam. "Best Summer Travel Destinations." WalletHub. May 14, 2023. https://wallethub.com/edu/best-summer-travel-destinations/3792.

———. "Most Diverse Cities in the U.S. (2024)." WalletHub. Apr. 15, 2024. https://wallethub.com/edu/most-diverse-cities/12690.

Miner, Craig. *Uncloistered Halls: The Centennial History of Wichita State University.* Wichita State University, Endowment Association, 1995.

Mowreader, Ashley. "Report: Cost of College, Stress Pushes Students to Consider Stopping Out." *Inside Higher Ed*, Apr. 18, 2024. https://www.insidehighered.com/news/student-success/health-wellness/2024/04/18/why-college-students-drop-out-school-and-what-can.

———. "Survey: Why Students Enroll and Why They Persist." *Inside Higher Ed*, Feb. 23, 2024. https://www.insidehighered.com/news/student-success/academic-life/2024/02/23/student-survey-gauges-importance-college-degree.

National Center for Science and Engineering Statistics. "Higher Education Research and Development (HERD) Survey." 2023. https://ncses.nsf.gov/surveys/higher-education-research-development/2022.

———. "Higher Education Research and Development (HERD) Survey." 2024. https://ncses.nsf.gov/surveys/higher-education-research-development/2023.

National Institute for Aviation Research. "About." Wichita State University. Accessed Apr. 2, 2025. https://www.wichita.edu/industry_and_defense/NIAR/about-us.php.

"Non-Discrimination." WSU Tech. 2024. https://wsutech.edu/nondiscrimination/.

Ogden, Charles. "I think this is a fantastic opportunity for students following a skilled-trades path." Facebook. Mar. 30, 2017. https://www.facebook.com/share/1Dw8e7mVgQ/.

Osterman, Michelle, Brady Hamilton, Joyce Martin, Anne Driscoll, and Claudia Valenzuela. "Births: Final Data for 2022." Centers for Disease Control. *National Vital Statistics Reports* 73, no. 2 (April 2024): 1–56.

Perez Tobias, Suzanne. "Wichita State, WATC Discussing Possible Expanded Affiliation or Merger." *The Wichita Eagle*, Oct. 21, 2015. https://www.kansas.com/news/local/education/article40529304.html.

———. "WSU Defends Koch-Funded Private School Being Built on Campus." *The Wichita Eagle*, Feb. 7, 2018. https://www.kansas.com/news/local/education/article198704414.html.

Pflugradt, Evan. "President John Bardo Discusses Shared Governance, Campus Changes." *The Sunflower*, Apr. 27, 2017. https://thesunflower.com/17548/news/president-john-bardo-discusses-shared-governance-campus-changes/.

"Programs of Study." WSU Tech. 2024. https://wsutech.edu/admissions/programs-of-study/.

"Public Institutions." Kansas Board of Regents. 2024. https://www.kansasregents.org/universities_colleges/public-institutions/public_institutions_accessible_list.

"Regional Growth Plan: An Economic Strategy for the Greater Wichita Region." Greater Wichita Partnership. Nov. 2018. https://greaterwichitapartnership.org/user/file/Regional%20Growth%20Plan%20Exec%20Summary_12.12.18.pdf.4/.

"Retired B-1B Arrives in Wichita to Create a Digital Twin." McConnell Air Force Base. Mar. 27, 2025. https://www.mcconnell.af.mil/News/Article/3659646/retired-b-1b-arrives-in-wichita-to-create-a-digital-twin/.

Roy, Bill, host. "Sheree Utash, Wichita Area Technical College." *BizTalk*. Podcast audio. Nov. 10, 2017. https://soundcloud.com/biztalkwiththewbj/episode-24-sheree-utash-wichita-area-technical-college.

Rydjord, John. *A History of Fairmount College*. Regents Press of Kansas, 1977.

Salazar, Daniel. "Bill Would Allow Technical College to Merge with Wichita State." *The Wichita Eagle*, Feb. 27, 2016. https://www.kansas .com/news/local/education/article62875372.html.

Shaw, Carolyn. "SEM Update—Oct. 22, 2021." Wichita State University. 2021. https://www.wichita.edu/academics/academic_affairs/SEM/sem _oct_21.php.

"Shocker Career Accelerator Annual Report 2022–2023." Wichita State University. 2024. https://my.visme.co/v/764rgd9z-yvqmjg.

"Shocker City Partnership." Wichita State University. 2024. https:// www.wichita.edu/services/accounts_receivable/ar_shocker_city _partnership.php.

"Shocker Select Tuition Discount." Wichita State University. 2024. https:// www.wichita.edu/admissions/undergraduate/tuition_programs /shocker_select.php.

Siebenmark, Jerry. "Airbus' Move to WSU Campus Brings Benefits Beyond New Building." *The Wichita Eagle*, Jan. 4, 2017. https://www .kansas.com/news/business/aviation/article124603509.html.

State Higher Education Executive Officers Association. "State Higher Education Finance Report: FY 2023." State Higher Education Finance. 2024. https://shef.sheeo.org/report/.

"States That Offer the Most Need-Based Scholarships and Grants." Scholaroo. Aug. 28, 2023. https://scholaroo.com/report/scholarships -and-grants-rankings/.

"Student Enrollment Factbook for Fall Census Day." Wichita State University. 2023. https://www.wichita.edu/services/planning_and _analysis/documents/Enrollment_Fall_Census_OPAweb.pdf.

Suellentrop, Paul. "Closing Braeburn Golf Course Ends an Era for Many Wichita Golfers." *The Wichita Eagle*, Aug. 20, 2014. https://www .kansas.com/news/article1258778.html.

———. "Wichita State Helps NASA Evaluate Possibilities for Life on Other Planets." Wichita State University. May 17, 2023. https://

www.wichita.edu/about/wsunews/news/2023/05-may/microbes
_3.php.

———. "Wichita State Is Now Home to a Nanosatellite, Taking Research
on NASA Project to a New Level." Wichita State University. July 11,
2024. https://www.wichita.edu/about/wsunews/news/2024/07-july
/cubesat_3.php.

———. "Wichita State Students Benefit from Applied Learning at Help
Hangar." Wichita State University. Mar. 16, 2019. https://www.wichita
.edu/about/wsunews/news/2019/03-march/helphangar.php.

"Suspenders4hope." Wichita State University. Accessed Mar. 7, 2025.
https://suspenders4hope.com/.

Swaim, Chance. "Faculty Senate Letter Confirmed, Sent to President
Bardo." The Sunflower, Mar. 16, 2017. https://thesunflower.com/15
882/news/faculty-senate-letter-confirmed-sent-to-president-bardo/.

Tague, Angela. "10 Best Metros for First-Time Home Buyers." Zillow.
Feb. 2, 2023. https://www.zillow.com/learn/best-cities-for-first-time
-home-buyers/.

Tank Ornelas, Sara. "Beyond the Classroom: Alia Michaelis." Wichita State University.May 23, 2022. https://www.wichita.edu/about
/wsunews/news/2022/05-may/michaelis_2.php.

———. "Digital Twin Program Brings New Life to Old Aircraft." Wichita State University. July 8, 2020. https://www.wichita.edu/about
/wsunews/news/2020/07-july/digital-twin_9.php.

———. "Engineers Without Borders Building Much-Needed Bridge for
Ecuadorian Village." Wichita State University. Aug. 28, 2023. https://
www.wichita.edu/about/wsunews/news/2023/08-aug/ewb_2.php.

———. "Treatment for Burn Wounds Could Be Revolutionized Through
Wichita State Research." Wichita State University. Feb. 8, 2023.
https://www.wichita.edu/about/wsunews/news/2023/02-feb/burn
wound_3.php.

———. "Wichita State Archaeologists Dig In to Unearth Cultural History." Wichita State University. Nov. 8, 2021. https://www.wichita.edu
/about/wsunews/news/2021/11-nov/cityarchaeologist_3.php.

———. "Wichita State Celebrates Opening of High-Volume COVID-19

Test Lab." Wichita State University. Oct. 19, 2020. https://www.wichita
.edu/about/wsunews/news/2020/10-oct/MDLopening_9.php.

———. "Wichita State Professor Wins Innovation Award to Create Accessible Comic Book App." Wichita State University. Feb. 3, 2021.
https://www.wichita.edu/about/wsunews/news/2021/02-feb/vizling
_3.php.

———. "Wichita State Researchers Aim to Educate, Protect Refugees
from Cyber-Scams." Wichita State University. June 20, 2022. https://
www.wichita.edu/about/wsunews/news/2022/06-jun/refugees
_3.php.

———. "WSU Lab That Took Off During COVID Switches Gears to
Microbiology." Wichita State University. April 6, 2023. https://www
.wichita.edu/about/wsunews/news/2023/04-april/MDLBeyond
Covid_3.php.

———. "WSU Researchers Win $1.4 Million NSF Grant to Mitigate En-
vironmental Impact of Road Salt." Wichita State University. Sept. 15,
2022.    https://www.wichita.edu/about/wsunews/news/2022/09-sept
/roadsalt_3.php.

———. "WSU's Gateway to IP Program Leads STEM Students into Patent Law Careers." Wichita State University. May 3, 2023. https://www
.wichita.edu/about/wsunews/news/2023/05-may/gateway_2.php.

Tanner, Beccy. "Grand Opening of Wichita State's Swanky Shocker Hall
Marks a New Era." *The Wichita Eagle*, June 16, 2015. https://www
.kansas.com/news/local/education/article1226167.html.

———. "WSU President Don Beggs to Retire at the End of June." *The
Wichita Eagle*, Sept. 27, 2011. https://www.kansas.com/news/local
/article1071129.html.

"2012 Strategic Planning Retreat." Wichita State University. 2012.
https://www.wichita.edu/about/strategic_plan/retreat_categories
/index.php.

United States Census Bureau. "Annual Estimates of the Resident Population for Incorporated Places in Kansas: April 1, 2020 to July 1,
2022." 2023.

———. "Historical Population Change Data (1910–2020)." Apr. 26, 2021.

https://www.census.gov/data/tables/time-series/dec/popchange
-data-text.html.

———. "QuickFacts: Wichita City, Kansas." July 1, 2024. https://www
.census.gov/quickfacts/fact/table/wichitacitykansas/PST045224.

University Faculty Senate. "Minutes from the General Faculty Meeting." Wichita State University. May 5, 2017. https://www.wichita.edu
/academics/facultysenate/Mgenfac5517.php.

Utash, Sheree. "It's Official: WATC Will Become the WSU Campus of
Applied Sciences and Technology." News release. WSU Tech. Accessed Dec. 12, 2024.https://wsutech.edu/archived/official-watc-will
-become-wsu-campus-applied-sciences-technology/.

Voorhis, Dan. "Wichita State's New Engineering Building Opens on
Innovation Campus." *The Wichita Eagle*, Jan. 18, 2017. https://www
.kansas.com/news/business/article127344084.html.

Walker, Jordan. "Quality education doesn't have to mean a traditional
four year degree." Facebook. Mar. 30, 2017. https://www.facebook
.com/share/p/1GFvEra75j/.

Wenzl, Roy. "New Wichita State Scholarship Program Aims to Boost Enrollment." *The Wichita Eagle*, Aug. 6, 2014. https://www.kansas.com
/article1125336.html.

———. "Wichita State Hires Recruiting Firm to Boost Enrollment."
*The Wichita Eagle*, Aug. 6, 2014. https://www.kansas.com/news
/article1123568.html.

White, Kevin. "WSU Announces Airbus to Build on Innovation Campus." KSNW-TV. Mar. 24, 2015. https://www.ksn.com/news/wsu
-announces-airbus-to-build-on-innovation-campus/.

"Whose University Is It Anyway?" Paid political advertisement. *The
Wichita Eagle*, Apr. 15, 2018.

Wial, Howard. "Interactive: Locating American Manufacturing." Brookings. May 9, 2012. https://www.brookings.edu/articles/interactive
-locating-american-manufacturing/.

"Wichita Biomedical Campus." Wichita State University. May 8, 2024.
https://www.wichita.edu/academics/wichita_biomedical_campus
/index.php.

"Wichita State Innovation Campus Aims to Unite University and Community." *Silicon Prairie News*, Jan. 5, 2016. https://siliconprairienews.com/2016/01/wichita-state-innovation-campus-aims-to-unite-university-and-community/.

"Wichita State Innovation Partner: Deloitte's Smart Factory @ Wichita." Wichita State University. Mar. 13, 2023. https://www.wichita.edu/about/wsunews/news/2023/03-march/smartfactory_4.php.

"Wichita State University." Carnegie Classification of Institutions of Higher Education. Accessed Mar. 31, 2025. https://carnegieclassifications.acenet.edu/institution/wichita-state-university/.

"Wichita State University." Graduate Criminal Justice Program Overview. *U.S. News and World Report*. Accessed Dec. 10, 2024. https://www.usnews.com.

"Wichita State University Announces Death of John Bardo, WCU Chancellor from 1995–2011." Western Carolina University. Mar. 13, 2019. https://www.wcu.edu/stories/posts/News/2019/03/wichita-state-university-announces-death-of-john-bardo-wcu-chancellor-from-1995-2011/index.aspx.

"Wichita State University Becoming an Innovation-Focused University." *Newswise*, Aug. 20, 2014) https://www.newswise.com/articles/wichita-state-university-becoming-an-innovation-focused-university.

"Wichita State University Honors College Charter." Wichita State University. Dec. 2, 2014. https://www.wichita.edu/academics/honors_college/documents/college_charter.pdf.

"Wichita State University Strategic Plan." Strategic Planning Steering Committee, Wichita State University. 2013. http://hdl.handle.net/10057/13046.

"Wichita State, WSU Tech Celebrate Highest Historical Enrollments." Wichita State University. Sept. 27, 2023. https://www.wichita.edu/about/wsunews/news/2023/09-sept/enrollment_1.php.

WSU News. "Wichita State Accepts Invitation to Join American Athletic Conference." Wichita State University. Apr. 7, 2017. https://www.wichita.edu/about/wsunews/news/2017/04-april/wsu_joins_aac.php.

WSU News Services. "New Online Teacher Apprentice Program Will Help Curb Teacher Shortage." Wichita State University. July 5, 2017. https://www.wichita.edu/about/wsunews/archive/index.php?nid =3662.

WSU Strategic Communications. "Air Force to Develop F-16 'Digital Twin' with Help from Wichita State NIAR." Wichita State University. June 30, 2021. https://www.wichita.edu/about/wsunews/news/2021 /06-jun/f-16_3.php.

———. "Experiential Engineering Building Will Be Renamed John Bardo Center." News release. Wichita State University. June 19, 2019. https://www.wichita.edu/about/wsunews-releases/2019/06-jun /bardo_center_release.php.

———. "New Wichita State Partnership with WSU Tech and Butler Will Help Critical Teacher Shortage." Wichita State University. July 5, 2023.    https://www.wichita.edu/about/wsunews/news/2023/07-july /cas_pathway_2.php.

———. "NIAR Announces New Partnerships for Boeing 777 Conversion Program." Wichita State University. Sept. 29, 2020. https://www .wichita.edu/about/wsunews-releases/2020/09-sept/boeing_777 _conversion_9.php.

———. "NIAR Engages Federal Grants to Accelerate Growth of Advanced Materials and Manufacturing." News release. Wichita State University. Oct. 18, 2023. https://www.wichita.edu/about/wsunews -releases/2023/10-oct/advanced_manufacturing_release_3.php.

———. "Wichita State's Record-Breaking Enrollment Driven by Access and Affordability." Wichita State University. Oct. 2, 2024. https://www .wichita.edu/about/wsunews/news/2024/10-oct/2024enrollment _1.php.

———. "WSU Awarded $51 Million to Advance Smart Manufacturing in South Kansas." News release. Wichita State University. Sept. 2, 2022. https://www.wichita.edu/about/wsunews-releases/2022/08 -aug/build_back_better_award_4.php.

———. "WSU to Help Modernize and Replace USAF's 'Nightwatch' Presidential Emergency Command Center Aircraft Fleet."

Wichita State University. Dec. 3, 2024. https://www.wichita.edu/about
/wsunews/news/2024/12-dec/nightwatch_story_3.php.

———. "WSU Strategic Plan." Wichita State University. 2023, 2024.
https://www.wichita.edu/about/strategic_plan/index.php.

"WSU Topics: Get to Know WSU Tech." Wichita State University.
Last updated May 2, 2019. https://www.wichita.edu/about/public
_information/wsu_topics/topics_wsu_tech.php.

Wu, Titus. "Kansas' COVID-19 Testing Capacity Finally Seeing a Boost,"
*The Topeka Capital-Journal*, Dec. 31, 2020, https://www.cjonline
.com/story/news/coronavirus/2020/12/31/kansas-covid-19-testing
-capacity-finally-seeing-boost/4065409001/.

"WuShock: A True Original." Wichita State University. Accessed Apr. 2,
2025, https://www.wichita.edu/about/wushock.php.

# Index

· · · · · · · · · · · · · · · · · · · · · · · · · · · · · · · · · · · · · · · · · · · · · · · · · · · · · ·

www.ingramcontent.com/pod-product-compliance
Lightning Source LLC
Chambersburg PA
CBHW020354100426
42812CB00001B/52

* 9 7 8 0 7 0 0 6 4 0 6 5 2 *